INTRODUCTION

At the 1939 New York World's Fair, visitors lined up for hours just to get a glimpse of a machine that seemed the ultimate scientific miracle. Big and boxy, it was something like their beloved radios at home—but with one huge difference. Right up there in front was a tiny screen—like a little movie screen—and every time a sound came from the machine a picture accompanied it! It was called television, which meant "seeing at a distance," and it was a fantastic little theater you could fit right in your home. Scientists had been working on the idea of television for almost fifty years, and as early as 1882 a French cartoonist had drawn his concept of what a television machine might look like. But now scientists were saying that this invention would soon be ready for general public consumption.

The wait turned out to be longer than expected. World War II intervened, and manufacturing of just about everything not essential to the war was halted.

The production of television for home use finally began in 1945. Only a hundred TV sets were manufactured in that first memorable year, and only people who'd been on the pre-war waiting lists got them. But more were promised, and a war-weary public was quick to vie for the sets as they came off the assembly lines of reconverted war factories.

If your family was lucky enough to be the first on the block to get a TV set, your house became the most envied in the neighborhood. Long-lost friends, relatives and neighbors suddenly began to appear on your doorstep, waiting for an invitation to see anything, and I mean anything, that happened to be on the TV. But if you were one of those poor unfortunates who were destined to become the last family on the block to get a TV set because you were determined to "wait until the prices go down" or were positive that TV was "just another passing fancy," you had to content yourself with putting on your best poor-little-waif act and, hat in hand, try to gain admittance to a neighbor's house which was more fortunately blessed with the wonders of TV.

TV-watching evenings were major social events in those days. There wasn't really much to view in those early days of TV, and telecasting was not a continuous all-day affair. Children's programs, cooking shows, amateurish variety offerings—people would sit for hours, viewing it all, even the TV test patterns, fascinated and totally spellbound.

3

Programs were mostly live then, and the shows, as well as the news events, all seemed vividly alive. Plays and politics, crime and comedy transformed our modest abodes into enchanted castles with little windows looking out over new and vast horizons. Little did we know then what these little windows would do to our lives. Never again would home provide us with sanctuary from the horrors and happenings of the outside world. Now we would be on hand at Senate subcommittee meetings and crime hearings, at public tragedies and coronations. Faces in the news would become as familiar to us as our favorite movie stars. Things were changing fast, and we would be able to sit and watch it all happen on our TV screens. Hot wars, like the one we had just lived through, would give way to cold wars, fought with words instead of on battlefields. New stars, television stars, began to take the spotlight away from movie and radio idols. Milton Berle, or Uncle Miltie as he was known to thousands of viewers, became television's King of Comedy. Howdy Doody, Sid Caesar and Imogene Coca, Kukla, Fran and Ollie and Captain Video became household names. Dramatic shows, telecast live, gave us more heroes to worship. The whole country became television-conscious. Soon old radio favorites like *The Lux Theatre, My Friend Irma,* Arthur Godfrey's *Talent Scouts, The Goldbergs, Your Hit Parade* and *Superman* made their moves from a sound world of radio to the sighted one of television with varying degrees of success, and early television broadcasting owed a large debt of gratitude to radio for some of its early offerings. But TV was more than old radio shows made visual. Programs were developed exclusively for television. Puppet shows like *Howdy Doody, Kukla, Fran and Ollie* and *Lucky Pup* and "magazines of the air" shows like *Omnibus, See It Now* and *Garroway at Large* were uniquely suited to the new medium of television.

The late 1940's and early 1950's became television's years of experimentation and discovery. It was during this time that TV developed a social conscience. It was television, for example, that was to expose the methods of Joseph McCarthy and thereby stem his rise. We saw dramatic art, civilized entertainment and intellectual exploration that haven't been duplicated for a decade. These were exciting years, perhaps the best that television has known and here is a chance to pause for a moment and look back over that older time as recalled by those old TV programs.

We begin in 1947, when television was still attempting to find itself, and then move into the 1950's, TV's "golden years," ending with 1958, the year when TV taping and the virtual disappearance of most live telecasting, except for the news shows, began to change the medium. Though in reality such a short time ago, those early TV years take on a quality of genuine nostalgia now, perhaps because we have advanced so far and so fast in such a relatively short span of years. I've tried to cram into this book of memories most of the top TV shows, specials and newsworthy events, but if one of your favorite TV happenings is missing from these pages, I only hope another old friend will make up for that omission. Come along then to the late 1940's and 1950's, and remember television . . . .

*(Major TV news headlines . . .
What was happening in the world . . .)*

1947

WW II VETS DEMAND NEW HOUSING
. . . . PRESIDENT ANNOUNCES TRUMAN
DOCTRINE, GIVING MILITARY AID TO
GREECE AND TURKEY . . . . EAST-WEST
TENSIONS INCREASE . . . . CONGRESS
ADOPTS MARSHALL PLAN . . . .
COMMUNIST COUP IN HUNGARY . . . .
TAFT-HARTLEY LAW PASSES SENATE,
OVERRIDING TRUMAN'S VETO . . . .

. . . and what was happening on TV . . .

Howdy and Buffalo Bob.

Howdy Doody, one of television's longest-running and best-remembered children's shows, began telecasting on December 27, 1947, and did not vacate its NBC habitat until thirteen years later in 1960.

The show's circus-puppet-theater setting was just the right atmosphere to capture kids' imaginations and keep them glued to the TV screen. Host Buffalo Bob Smith; Howdy, the cowboy-marionette; horn-honking speechless Clarabel the Clown; Indian princess Summer-Fall-Winter-Spring; puppet Mr. Bluster and his pal, Flubberdub, became weekday favorite visitors to millions of American households. The demand for tickets to attend a live telecast of the show was so overwhelming that NBC had an endless waiting list of youngsters whose fondest dream was to appear on camera with their *Howdy Doody* friends.

HOWDY DOODY

THEME SONG: (To the tune of Ta-Ra-Ra-Boom-De-Ay)

It's Howdy Doody time.
It's Howdy Doody time.
Bob Smith and Howdy too
Say Howdy—do to you.
Let's give a rousing cheer,
For Howdy Doody's here.
It's time to start the show.
So, kids, let's go!

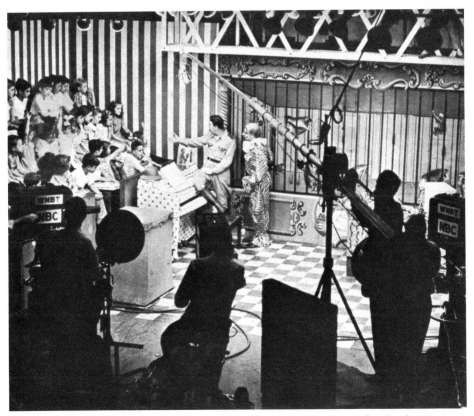

Buffalo Bob and Clarabel talk to the Peanut Gallery during a *Howdy Doody* telecast.

John F. Kennedy, then a U.S. Senator, is seen (above) with *Kraft* floor manager, Ken Lynch, going over the script of a tele-adaptation of *Profiles in Courage*, which was presented on the *Kraft Theatre* in 1956.

Restoration classics like *She Stoops to Conquer* were standard fare on *Kraft Theatre*. Margaret Phillips, Louise Prussing, Leon Shaw and Ralph Nelson are seen (above) during this 1948 telecast.

Ossie Davis and Everett Sloane starred in the 1955 *Kraft* presentation of *The Emperor Jones* by Eugene O'Neill.

KRAFT THEATRE

The Kraft Theatre, an hour-long series of weekly live dramatic productions, began as a local show in New York in 1947 and graduated to the big time as a national nighttime program in 1948. During the series' eleven-year residency on NBC, such diversified plays and players as *The Glove,* starring TV's busiest leading lady of the late 1940's—early 1950's, Margaret Phillips; *The Emperor Jones,* with black actor Ossie Davis; and John F. Kennedy's *Profiles in Courage* were presented. Although the show concentrated mainly on proved stage successes and adaptations of classic novels and plays, original plays, expressly written for television, were occasionally offered as well.

One of *Kraft Theatre's* best-received productions was the dramatization of the popular novel *A Night to Remember*, which was about the sinking of the *Titanic*.

PAUL WINCHELL   AND   JERRY MAHONEY

Ventriloquist Paul Winchell with his dummy Jerry Mahoney was one of the first variety entertainers to have a regular show on television. As early as 1947 Winchell made his video debut in a show of his own, which was called *Show Business, Inc.* In 1948, he co-starred with master mind reader Dunninger on NBC's *The Bigelow Show.* Winchell then went on to *The Speidel Show,* serving as MC from 1951 until 1953. In 1953 he picked up Jerry, Knucklehead Smith, and all the rest of his dummy friends and moved to a daytime spot, hosting a popular children's program which featured fun talk, games and a fair sprinkling of film cartoons to keep the small fry at home happy.

Jerry Mahoney and his master, Paul Winchell.

MEET THE PRESS

Television's most durable panel-news-discussion program, *Meet the Press,* presided over by Martha Rountree, made a successful transition from radio to television in 1947. Guest newspapermen questioned leaders of the political scene, with Miss Rountree and later Ned Brooks acting as moderator. This long-running show, still going strong, was produced by Lawrence E. Spivak.

Representatives of the press (above) "meet" Alexander de Seversky. Martha Rountree sits at his right.

THE ROLLER DERBY

Tuffy Brasuhn takes a tumble.

The rough-and-ready *Roller Derby* was a favorite evening sports attraction for millions of viewers during television's early years. The collision of human bodies, knock-down-drag-out fights—especially among the ladies—provided more entertainment than the incredibly swift skating. Tuffy Brasuhn, the toughest tomato on skates, became a household name and attracted a considerable following during her long career with the Derby. Blond bombshell Mary Gardner ran her a close second.

The looks on these skaters' faces show just how seriously competitors took the Derby.

Gorgeous George looks perplexed.

Mr. America—Gene Stanlee.

Dennis James, at ringside, watches the countdown.

WRESTLING

One of the most popular attractions during television's childhood were the nightly telecasts of wrestling matches. Few viewers can forget the ringside manner of Dennis James, wrestling's most celebrated sportscaster, or the shenanigans of "Hatpin Mary," a wild old girl, who took special delight in sticking her unfavorite wrestlers with a deadly hatpin. Among the viewers' favorite wrestling performers were the Swedish Angel, The Zebra Kid, Gorgeous George, Mr. America, Ricki Starr and, of course, the biggest and best of them all, Antonino Rocca.

Also popular were the special lady wrestling events and midget wrestling. As the years rolled by, the wrestling matches became splashier and splashier—with contestants making grand entrances replete with entourages of slave girls, fan bearers and sedan chair carriers. No one seemed to take the matches seriously, however, since everyone knew that all the howling and grunting were being staged strictly for the benefit of the viewing audience. And watch they did, until the mid-1950's, when the novelty of it all wore off.

"Hatpin Mary" chats with James during a break in the matches.

THE GENE AUTRY SHOW

Gene Autry and his horse, Champion.

Among the first movie Western stars to discover the gold in television's hills was singing cowboy Gene Autry. He first appeared on television in his own weekly adventure series in 1947. Gene's Melody Ranch, his friend Pat Buttram, and his horse, Champion, became as popular on TV as they had been on radio and in motion pictures.

THE FIRST WORLD SERIES TELECAST

The first World Series game to be telecast.

Four cities were lucky enough to receive the first telecast of a World Series baseball game. It was played between the New York Yankees and the Brooklyn Dodgers, in 1947. The cities chosen for this special consideration were New York, Philadelphia, Washington and, of all places, Schenectady. The first game was played in old Ebbets Field in Brooklyn, the home of the Dodgers when they were still the Brooklyn "Bums." The winners? The Yankees . . . as usual.

"Hey, we're getting a television set tomorrow!" It was a happy cry that was to grow more and more familiar in the late 1940's. Those early sets were monstrous, with their huge cabinets and their one tiny eye that made them look like a nearsighted Cyclops. But to millions of people all over the country who had been waiting for television to become a reality all through the war years, they were the most beautiful pieces of machinery they had ever seen.

Only a **PHILCO** Radio-Phonograph Gives You This

Glorious Concert Hall Realism

This is it . . . utterly matchless perfection of tone as the great new Philco 1613 reproduces the sensational 45 minute records with glorious "Concert Hall" realism, thanks to the exclusive Philco Balanced Fidelity Reproducer. Present records are played automatically by a *second tone arm.* Yours with genuine Philco FM-AM radio, in classic-modern mahogany console.

When You're Ready for Television

Enjoy the sharpest, brightest, clearest picture in the industry . . . plus all the advantages that Philco pioneering research brings you . . . automatic tuning . . . Eye-Level viewing ease. Get all that's newest and best . . . buy Philco!

TUNE IN Philco Radio Time with Bing Crosby Wednesday evening . . . Philco Television Playhouse Sunday evening. See your newspaper for time and station.

No wonder Hollywood Picked G-E

In the exciting new Roy Del Ruth production—"The Babe Ruth Story"—William Bendix re-enacts that unforgettable moment in the 1932 World Series when the crowd-ridden Babe pointed to the upper stands at Wrigley Field and slammed the next pitch right in there for a home run.

Beats everything in sight!

GE DAYLIGHT TELEVISION

MODEL 810

TALK TO ANYBODY WHO'S SEEN IT! You're looking at the first low-priced table model with G-E Daylight Television. 52 sq. inches of unprecedented picture quality on the big 10 inch direct-view tube. All U. S. television channels, with factory pre-tuned circuits. One glance and you marvel at the "stand-out" superiority! When you see it, the price is even more marvelous. Model 810, only **$325.00*** *(Plus installation)*

Don't miss "The Babe Ruth Story" featuring the stirring television scene. To show the best in television, Hollywood naturally turned to General Electric. See G-E Daylight Television for yourself. G-E Television is performance-engineered at famous Electronics Park. It's the brightest, clearest TV picture ever delivered . . . *your eyes prove it!* You owe yourself and your family a thrilling demonstration. Ask your General Electric Television Dealer.

General Electric Company, Receiver Division, Electronics Park, Syracuse, N. Y.

GENERAL ELECTRIC
174-08

GIANT SCREEN-PROJECTION TELEVISION! De luxe television on a super-big screen. All the action on a dramatic picture 3 sq. ft. in area. Superb television plus FM radio, standard (AM) radio, plus short-wave radio, plus automatic phonograph with the famed G-E Electronic Reproducer. Showpiece period cabinet styled in, genuine mahogany. Model 901 . . . **$2100.00*** *(Plus installation)*

MODEL 901

* *Western prices slightly higher. Prices subject to change without notice.*

COMPLETE ENTERTAINMENT CENTER! G-E Daylight Television. FM radio. AM radio. Automatic phonograph with G-E Electronic Reproducer. Biggest combination "buy" on the market today. All the eye-arresting advantages of G-E Daylight Television on big 10" direct-view tube. Both radio and records in matchless G-E natural tone. All yours in Model 802D at only **$725.00*** *(Plus installation)*

MODEL 802D

32

Cooking shows were popular attractions on early television. Dione Lucas, seen above, was one of television's first cooking instructors to gain national attention.

1948

PRESIDENT BENES OF CZECHOSLO-
VAKIA FORCED TO YIELD TO COM-
MUNISTS . . . . EAST GERMANS BLOCK-
ADE BERLIN . . . . BIG ALLIED AIR LIFT
FEEDS WEST BERLINERS . . . . GOP
GOVERNOR DEWEY OF NEW YORK
LAUNCHES PRESIDENTIAL CAMPAIGN
. . . . TRUMAN RETURNED TO WHITE
HOUSE FOR FOUR MORE YEARS. DEM-
OCRATS WIN 247 HOUSE AND 54 SEN-
ATE SEATS . . . .

Television's first major star unquestionably was comedian Milton Berle. His *Texaco Star Theatre* became the most frequently looked-at, talked-about show on the air in the late 1940's and early 1950's. Tuesday night became "Milton Berle Night," and viewers lucky enough to own a TV set wouldn't miss a single fun-filled hour of "Uncle Miltie." They loved his impressive array of guest stars and his devotion to his mother, Sandra, and never knew what sort of crazy getup he would be wearing when he made his weekly entrance. Whether dressed in ladies' clothes, done up as Howdy Doody, or all decked out as a monster pumpkin pie, Miltie never failed to convulse his audience with jokes reportedly "stolen" from the best comedians in the business.

NBC was fortunate enough to have Mr. Berle's talents on display for eight years, from June, 1948, until June, 1956.

The end of a night with "Uncle Miltie" shows guests, Phil Silvers, Buffalo Bob Smith, June Havoc and Clarabel the Clown flanking Milton, dressed up as Howdy Doody.

TEXACO STAR THEATRE

Mr. Television.

HOPALONG CASSIDY

Bill Boyd as Hopalong Cassidy.

In 1948, screen-serial cowboy Bill Boyd joined television's roster of new stars. His celebrated Hopalong Cassidy motion-picture character made the series an immediate success with youngsters across the nation and became TV's first big Western hit. After one year on the air, Mr. Boyd hocked all his belongings, lock, stock and barrel, to buy the Hopalong TV rights from its film-producer owners. When he finally sold out several years later, he reportedly received $70,000,000! Reruns of *Hopalong Cassidy* are still being shown on many local networks.

ARTHUR GODFREY'S TALENT SCOUTS

Arthur Godfrey was the host of CBS' *Talent Scouts* program from 1948 into the 1950's. Each week famous show-business names would introduce Arthur to new acts they had discovered, thus giving unknowns the chance to display their talents before a fast-growing TV public. Weekly winners were chosen by an applause meter. Most of Godfrey's "friends," who costarred with him on his *Arthur Godfrey and His Friends* weekly hour-long variety show, were former *Talent Scouts* winners. The show had a long and healthy ten-year run on CBS.

Arthur samples a cup of Lipton's Tea, longtime sponsor of *Talent Scouts*. Viewers often wondered whether Arthur's teacup contained something other than tea.

The *Talent Scouts'* famous applause meter.

TV's highest paid guest star . . . Elvis Presley.

Gospel singer Mahalia Jackson made her TV debut on the Sullivan show.

Ed introduced many comics to the TV viewing public. One of their favorites proved to be comedian Jack Carter.

THE TOAST OF THE TOWN

America's favorite variety show, *The Ed Sullivan Show*, was originally called *The Toast of the Town* when it first arrived on television. Dour-faced, unsmiling newspaper columnist Sullivan first told his home viewers that he had a "really big shew" for them on June 20, 1948. He has been a Sunday-night favorite ever since. Many well-known entertainers made their TV debuts on the Sullivan show. Ed's first *Toast of the Town* featured the little-known comedy team of Dean Martin and Jerry Lewis in their first TV showcasing. Since then, Ed has introduced such now-famous entertainers as Alan King, Jackie Mason, The Beatles, Victor Borge and Margaret Truman. The hip-shaking rock-and-roll rage of the 1950's, Elvis Presley, was paid the highest price, a record $50,000 for a single guest appearance on Ed's show. Julia Meade assisted Ed as cohostess and chief product seller during and for a while after his *Toast of the Town* years. Ed has been on the air for more than twenty years.

Ed Sullivan and Julia Meade.

The cast of *The Toast of the Town*'s first program line up on stage at the end of the show.

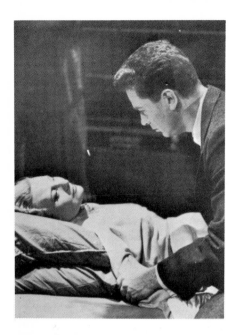

Michele Morgan and Arthur Franz starred in a modern-dress version of the classic *Camille* in 1953.

Judith Evelyn and Charlton Heston costarred in *Studio One*'s 1951 adaptation of Shakespeare's *Macbeth*.

English funny lady Gracie Fields appeared with Janet Swanson in *Mrs. 'Arris Goes to Paris* in 1958.

Shakespeare's *Julius Caesar*, with Alfred Ryder and Shepperd Strudwick, was presented in 1955.

STUDIO ONE

Television's longest-running, best-remembered dramatic anthology series, *Studio One*, was first telecast over the CBS network in 1948. Originating live from New York, the show presented such outstanding hour-long teleplays as Reginald Rose's *Twelve Angry Men, The Kill* with Grace Kelly, *Mrs. 'Arris Goes to Paris* with English comedienne Gracie Fields, Shakespeare's *Macbeth* with Charlton Heston and Judith Evelyn, *Julius Caesar*, also with Heston, *Camille* with French actress Michele Morgan, and TV's first modern-dress Shakespeare production, *Coriolanus*. Some of TV's most successful playwrights began their careers writing for *Studio One*. Until the show's final telecast, in 1957, it remained the public's favorite dramatic show.

Leo Coleman and Marie Powers starred in a 1948 hour-long opera, *The Medium*, by Gian Carlo Menotti.

THE LONE RANGER

The masked rider of the plains, the Lone Ranger, proved as popular on television as he had been on his long-running radio series. One of the earliest Western shows to find its way to television, *The Lone Ranger* brought its famous introduction right along with it from radio:

"A fiery horse with the speed of light, a cloud of dust and a hearty hi-yo Silver. The Lone Ranger!"

"With his faithful Indian companion, Tonto, the masked rider of the plains led the fight for law and order in the early Western United States. Nowhere in the pages of history can one find a greater champion of justice. Return with us now to those thrilling days of yesteryear. From out of the past come the thundering hoofbeats of the great horse Silver. The Lone Ranger rides again!"

The TV version of *The Lone Ranger* starred Clayton Moore as the Ranger and Jay Silverheels, a real-life Indian, as Tonto. They are seen above with Silver.

THE ORIGINAL AMATEUR HOUR

Major Bowes' radio showcase for amateur talent, *The Original Amateur Hour*, was an early television hit. With Ted Mack replacing a deceased Major Bowes as host of the series, jugglers, singers and spoon players were placed in weekly competition with one another for top honors. Winners were decided by an applause meter and by phone calls and mail from home viewers. The show has been on the air continuously since 1948, finding its way to all three major networks at one time or another.

The Original Amateur Hour's **host, Ted Mack.**

LUCKY PUP

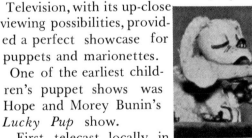

Lucky Pup

Television, with its up-close viewing possibilities, provided a perfect showcase for puppets and marionettes.

One of the earliest children's puppet shows was Hope and Morey Bunin's *Lucky Pup* show.

First telecast locally in New York in 1948, the show became immensely popular with young viewers, and its show's "stars," Pup, Pinhead and Foodini, became celebrities.

Puppeteers Hope and Morey Bunin work their creations, Pinhead and Foodini.

29

Betty Field and Efrem Zimbalist, Jr., in *Street Scene*.

Frances Reid, José Ferrer and Paula Lawrence appeared in the 1949 *Philco Playhouse* production of *Cyrano de Bergerac*.

Judith Evelyn starred as Camille in 1948.

PHILCO PLAYHOUSE

TV producer Fred Coe presented a weekly dramatic series in 1948 on NBC called the *Philco Playhouse*. The show, after two years on its own, began alternating on a biweekly basis with *The Goodyear Playhouse,* also produced by Mr. Coe, from 1951 to 1955. During *Philco*'s long and distinguished television run, Mr. Coe drew heavily upon the writing talents of such notable TV playwrights as Paddy Chayefsky and Rod Serling. Among the productions and stars presented on the show were Judith Evelyn in *Camille*, Joanne Woodward and Kim Stanley in *Young Lady of Property*, Lillian Gish in *The Late Christopher Bean*, Alfred Drake in *Quality Street*, John Baragrey in *Pride and Prejudice* and José Ferrer in *Cyrano de Bergerac.* Mr. Ferrer's TV performance as Cyrano proved so successful that he repeated it in a motion picture that won him an Academy Award.

Philco Playhouse's host and sometimes star, Bert Lytell.

Philco's 1948 version of *The Old Lady Shows Her Medals* starred Cameron Mitchell and Lucile Watson.

Unknowns Joanne Woodward and Kim Stanley appeared together in *Young Lady of Property*.

31

ONE OF THE TRULY GREAT

NEEDS NO AERIAL—brings in beautifully clear sharp picture in all normal locations without an aerial of any kind, on a huge 97 square inch screen. Has the exclusive Philco luxury feature — the No-Glare Optical System that eliminates glare, makes television, at last, *easy on your eyes!* The new, exclusive Philco 3-speed automatic phonograph plays all kinds of records of all sizes, at all speeds automatically. You get more than 5 hours of continuous music. And the new Philco Super-Tone reproducer exerts just 1/5 ounce needle pressure on your records — gives you the finest tone ever achieved for recorded music. Plus the new Philco Super-powered AM-FM radio. All in a distinguished modern cabinet with full-length doors. Philco model 1479.

$499⁹⁵
Tax and Warranty $11.75
Price slightly higher in far West

NEEDS NO AERIAL. New Philco Electronic Built-In Aerial gives sensational performance in a normal location. 97 square inch picture. 2-way automatic phonograph for Long Playing and regular records, and new Philco super-powered AM-FM radio. Almost $300.00 less than last year. Model 1477.

$399⁹⁵
Tax and Warranty $9.75

THE GREAT NEW
1950 PHILCOS
cost as much as
$200⁰⁰ LESS
than last year.. and now
the <u>advertised</u> price
is the <u>final</u> price...
nothing else to buy

NEEDS NO AERIAL in any normal location. New Philco super-sensitive television circuit and High Gain Tuner give you a clearer and sharper picture than ever on a huge 97 square inch screen. No high cost installation, and the price is nearly $200.00 less than last year's 90 square inch picture. Philco model 1400.

$259⁹⁵
Tax and Warranty $3.80

24

(News of the world . . .)

1949

TRUMAN ANNOUNCES POINT FOUR PROGRAM OF ECONOMIC AID TO UNDERDEVELOPED COUNTRIES . . . . NATO FORMED TO STRENGTHEN WESTERN ALLIANCE . . . . BLIZZARD HITS NORTHEASTERN UNITED STATES . . . . NATIONAL HOUSING ACT PROVIDES FOR SLUM CLEARANCE . . . . RUSSIA ANNOUNCES IT HAS A BOMB . . . . MAO TSE-TUNG FORMS PEOPLE'S REPUBLIC OF CHINA . . . .

. . . and what was on TV that year . . .

LIFE WITH RILEY

A younger, much slimmer Jackie Gleason played Riley, and Rosemary De Camp played his wife, Peg, in the 1949 version of *The Life of Riley*. Gloria Winters played their daughter, Babs.

William Bendix, Marjorie Reynolds, Lugene Sanders and Wesley Morgan appeared as the Riley family in the 1953 version of the show.

Before he became the celebrated star of a variety series on television, rotund comedian Jackie Gleason appeared as Chester Riley in a 1949 situation comedy series called *The Life of Riley*. Costarring with Gleason as his wife, Peg, was Rosemary De Camp. The series lasted only one season on the NBC network, but three years later, in 1953, the show was returned to the airwaves, this time starring William Bendix as Riley and Marjorie Reynolds as Peg. Wesley Morgan appeared as their son, Junior, and Lugene Sanders their daughter, Babs. Gloria Blondell and Tom D'Andrea played their friends and neighbors Gillis and Honeybee. This time the show remained on the air for five years.

MAMA

The weekly adventures of an immigrant Norwegian family living in San Francisco at the turn of the century, which was presented by CBS from 1949 to 1957, were a viewing must for millions. *Mama* starred Peggy Wood in the title role and featured Judson Laire as Papa, Dick Van Patten as their son, Nels, Rosemary Rice and Robin Morgan as their daughters, Katrin and Dagmar. Based on a novelette, *Mama's Bank Account*, by Kathryn Forbes and a subsequent play, *I Remember Mama* by John Van Druten, the *Mama* series was a long-standing favorite. In 1956, when CBS canceled the show, public clamor was such that it was brought back for another year.

The Hanson family: Nels (Dick Van Patten), Katrin (Rosemary Rice), Dagmar (Robin Morgan) and, standing, Papa (Judson Laire) and Mama (Peggy Wood).

MARTIN KANE, PRIVATE EYE

No fewer than four famous actors played the title role of *Martin Kane, Private Eye* during its five-year run on NBC-TV. Lloyd Nolan was the first Kane; Mark Stevens, the second; William Gargan, who had played the role on radio, the third; and stage star Lee Tracy, the fourth. The series lasted longer than most adventure-crime offerings, perhaps because each season a new star was brought in to keep up audience interest.

Radio's Martin Kane, William Gargan, repeating the role on television.

PANTOMIME QUIZ

Mike Stokey's *Pantomime Quiz* was one of television's earliest game-panel show hits. First telecast on October 4, 1949, the show played the old parlor game of charades. It remained on CBS from 1949 to 1954, when it switched its home base to the ABC network. There it remained until 1958, when it went the local-station syndication route. Stokey remained the show's MC throughout the entire national run of the series, and some of the celebrities who performed on the show were Hans Conried, Jackie Coogan, Una Merkel, Adele Jergens, Morey Amsterdam, and Beverly Garland.

Musical comedy star Gretchen Wyler was an ofttime guest on *Pantomime Quiz*. She is seen here with MC Stokey.

MAN AGAINST CRIME

The well-known star of stage and motion pictures Ralph Bellamy added dignity to the *Man Against Crime* series, an early CBS crime show. Mr. Bellamy played the Mike Barnett role from 1949 to 1953. After a three-year absence from television, the series returned with former radio and movie actor Frank Lovejoy as Barnett. It remained on the air for another two years.

Ralph Bellamy as Mike Barnett, the "man against crime."

THE MAGIC CLOWN

A clever actor with the unusual name of Zovella played the part of Bonomo, the Magic Clown who, until 1954, delighted youngsters with his tricks, puppet wizardry and "giveaway prizes."

ROBERT MONTGOMERY PRESENTS

In the early years of commercial TV broadcasting, weekly live dramatic programs were popular attractions. One of the most successful anthology series of the time was Robert Montgomery's *Lucky Strike Theatre*. Each week, the movie actor and director would introduce and sometimes star in hour-long adaptations of well-known plays, books and original teleplays. Among the plays presented on this series were *The Hunchback of Notre Dame, Great Expectations, Onions in the Stew, Sunset Boulevard, The Lost Weekend* and *David Copperfield*. Midway in its seven-year run the show's title was changed to *Robert Montgomery Presents*.

Mr. Montgomery appeared in several of his *Robert Montgomery Presents* **plays. He is seen here with Susan Douglas in his production of** *Ride the Pink Horse.*

THE MAGIC COTTAGE

Pretty Pat Meikle was the hostess and TV teacher on *The Magic Cottage*, an early children's participation program. Miss Meikle was expert at story telling and her "magic cottage," where "everything and anything could happen," proved a pleasant whimsical setting for her readings, game playing and puppet shows.

Magic Cottage **hostess Pat Meikle.**

ONE MAN'S FAMILY

Radio's longest-running noninterrupted series, *One Man's Family*, was brought to television on November 4, 1949. Although the TV version of the serial did not have the longevity of the radio series (some thirty-odd years), the show attracted enough support to remain on the screen to April, 1951.

The television series, like its radio counterpart, told the story of the Barbour family of San Francisco. Father Barbour was played by Bert Lytell and Mother Barbour by Marjorie Gateson. Their children were played by Martin Dean, Ann Wallace, and Eva Marie Saint, who went on to star on the stage and in motion pictures.

Father Barbour (Bert Lytell), Claudia (Eva Marie Saint) and Mother Barbour (Marjorie Gateson) during a *One Man's Family* telecast.

THE HERB SHRINER SHOW

Television had its own Will Rogers in slow-talking country boy Herb "The Hoosier Hotshot" Shriner. Herb became one of television's earliest stars on his CBS show in 1949. By 1953 he'd become the host of a weekly quiz program, *Two for the Money*. In 1956 he returned to the variety-show format, but people didn't seem to be laughing as much as they had in 1949 at his particular brand of humor. The show was canceled before it completed one full season.

The star of *Two for the Money* and *The Herb Shriner Show*, Herb Shriner.

... opera's *Rigoletto* ...

Imogene and Sid as Samson and Delilah.

... ballet's *Afternoon of a Faun* ...

Mr. Caesar and Miss Coca spoof
From Here to Eternity.

... the Russians ...

YOUR SHOW OF SHOWS

Sid Caesar and Imogene Coca.

Every Saturday night in the late 1940's and early 1950's the big television show to watch was NBC's *Admiral Broadway Revue, Your Show of Shows,* which starred comedians Sid Caesar and Imogene Coca. Producer Max Liebman lavished tender loving care on each 90-minute broadcast. In the show's fourth year on TV its title was cut to *Your Show of Shows,* the name by which it is remembered by most TV viewers.

Sid and Imogene made their first appearance on the show in 1949. Their spoofs of old and foreign movies, their pantomimes and musical sketches became TV classics, and few viewers can forget their hilarious spoof of *From Here to Eternity* or their "Italian" movie gibberish.

Miss Coca and Mr. Caesar were surrounded each week by a talented cast of regulars—opera singer Marguerite Piazza; comic Carl Reiner, who supported the stars in various sketches; the dancing Hamilton Trio; singer Bill Hayes; the Billy Williams Quartet; and dancers Bambi Linn and Rod Alexander.

In 1954 the stars decided to go their separate ways. Neither of them was ever to be as wildly popular separately as they had been together.

PETER LIND HAYES
AND
MARY HEALY

The husband and wife team of Peter Lind Hayes and Mary Healy were early TV pioneers with their 1949 variety-talk show called *Inside U.S.A.* The following year they teamed up with nightclub owner Sherman Billingsley on *The Stork Club*, where they interviewed guest celebrities.

Mary Healy and Peter Lind Hayes with TV's famous chimp, J. Frederick Muggs.

ED WYNN

Vaudeville's "Perfect Fool," Ed Wynn, had talents which were tailor-made for TV, and CBS presented the indestructible funny man in his own comedy-variety show in 1949. After one year, Ed joined the *Four Star Revue* roster of weekly alternating stars. Still one year later, the show increased its roster of stars from four to more, Ed among them, and the show became known as *The All Star Revue*. In 1958 Ed surprised everyone by making his debut as a serious dramatic actor playing in such celebrated TV presentations as Rod Serling's *Requiem for a Heavyweight* and in the movie version of *The Diary of Anne Frank*. In the late 1950's Ed returned to television as the star of a half hour weekly situation comedy, but the show was not successful. Thereafter he confined his TV appearances to occasional guest spots on variety and dramatic offerings.

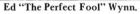
Ed "The Perfect Fool" Wynn.

THE GOLDBERGS

Lovable Jewish Mama Molly Goldberg, played by Gertrude Berg, brought her warmth and humor to TV in 1949. Following the same pattern used ever since the 1930's in the successful radio series, the show was an instant hit. Who can ever forget the familiar Bronx setting of the Goldbergs' apartment, Molly's gruff but practical husband, Jake, played by Phillip Loeb, her son, Sammy, and her daughter, Rosalie, played by Larry Robinson and Arlene McQuade, and her Uncle David, played by Eli Mintz.

Soon after it first appeared on the home screens, people were quoting Molly's wonderfully mixed-up expressions like "In the pot put the chicken" and "So who's to know?" Each week they squealed with delight as Molly leaned out of her kitchen window and called across the alley to her neighbor, "Yoo-hoo, Mrs. Cohen."

A Goldberg family portrait. Molly (Gertrude Berg) is surrounded by husband Jake (Phillip Loeb), daughter Rosalie (Arlene McQuade), and son Sammy (Larry Robinson).

CAPTAIN VIDEO

When television was still in its youth and most of the shows were live, a local New York telecast on the Dumont station caught viewers' attention. The show, *Captain Video*, with its makeshift scenery and inexpensive-looking props, starred former radio actor Al Hodge as the gallant Captain Video. Long Island teen-ager Don Hastings played the young Video Ranger.

Even though the show looked as if it were being telecast from someone's basement with its painted, cardboard-box-like spaceships and kiddy car controls, no one who watched TV in those early years would miss this science fiction unspectacular.

Captain Video (Al Hodge) and his Video Ranger (Don Hastings) inspect their ship controls.

ESPECIALLY FOR YOU

Pert TV singer Roberta Quinlan was the star of a fifteen-minute daily music show, *Especially for You*, from 1949 to 1956.

Roberta Quinlan accompanying herself at the piano.

GARROWAY AT LARGE

The Chicago-based *Garroway at Large* show, starring easy-mannered Dave Garroway, was an NBC favorite beginning in 1949. The show featured singers Connie Russell, Jack Haskell and comedian Cliff Norton and had a large TV following. Dave leisurely walked from set to set introducing songs, skits and guests. Then he moved on to New York, where he became the host of NBC's *Today* show, an early-morning news and special-features program.

Dave Garroway "chopping" the cable to close his show.

Frank Parker and Marion Marlowe.

Julius La Rosa and Janette Davis.

Haleloke and Godfrey dueting with their ukuleles.

ARTHUR GODFREY
AND
HIS FRIENDS

Popular Arthur Godfrey took his successful at-ease radio show before the CBS-TV cameras in 1949. He was already the host of CBS' *Talent Scouts* program and continued in this capacity. But his weekly hour-long variety-musical show soon became more popular than the *Scouts*, and his "friends"—singers Janette Davis, Bill Lawrence, Julius La Rosa, Marion Marlowe, The Mariners, LuAnn Simms, Carmel Quinn and the Maguire Sisters, along with The Chordettes—became almost as famous as Godfrey himself.

Feuds between Godfrey and his "friends" were soon making newspaper headlines, however, as was the way he sometimes fired a member of the cast right on camera. Arthur's ukulele playing, his gently critical commercial messages and his tales of plane piloting kept the show on the air until 1959, when he left for reasons of health.

Godfrey and the Maguire Sisters.

Fran Allison, Mercedes and Madame Oglepuss.

Burr Tillstrom, his puppets Kukla and Ollie, and
Fran Allison celebrated their seventh anniversary
on the air in 1954.

A *Kukla, Fran and Ollie* telecast.

KUKLA, FRAN AND OLLIE

One puppet TV show, which was probably enjoyed by as many adults as children was NBC's *Kukla, Fran and Ollie* show. Actress Fran Allison's conversations with Burr Tillstrom's cloth and plaster characters had everyone believing the puppets were flesh and blood. First seen on local television in Chicago in 1947, it became a national network show in 1949.

Gentle Kukla, with his high voice and round, bulbous nose; lovable Ollie the Dragon, with his good-natured conceit; busty, overbearing Madame Oglepuss; cantankerous Beulah the Witch; "Dumb" Cecil Bill and his "Do-De-Doi-Doi;" Windbag Colonel Crackie; Dolores Dragon, Ollie's niece; Mercedes and Fletcher

The Kuklapolitan Players, from left to right, Colonel Crackie, Cecil Bill, Mercedes, Kukla, Ollie, Madame Oglepuss, Beulah the Witch and Fletcher Rabbitt.

Rabbitt, all controlled and spoken for by master puppeteer Mr. Tillstrom, won a permanent place for themselves in the hearts of millions of Americans. One of the show's most popular features was the performances of plays and operettas by the Kuklapolitan Players, which included all the puppets and Miss Allison. When *Kukla, Fran and Ollie* was dropped in 1954, public demand for its return was so strong NBC brought back the show for another five years. Since 1957 Mr. Tillstrom and his puppets have been seen as guests on various variety shows and specials and can be seen on NET-TV. This show remains in the memories of the public as one of the classics of TV's Golden Age.

MR. I. MAGINATION

Each weekday young television fans paid a visit to *Mr. I. Magination*'s "Imagination Town." From April, 1949, to June, 1952, youngsters could have "their every wish come true" in this magical town, created just for them by Mr. I. Magination himself, Paul Tripp. Stories, games, songs and crafts were the daily order of business in Imagination Town.

Mr. I. Magination—Paul Tripp.

SUPER CIRCUS

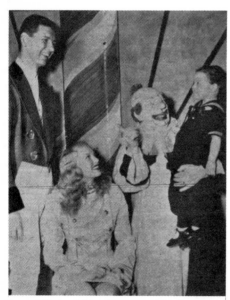

A very popular show for kids was *Super Circus*, which was presented by ABC from 1949 to 1956. The regular circus troupe that appeared on the show included ringmaster Claude Kirchner; clowns Cliffy, the tramp, Scampy, the boy clown, and Nick Francis, the fat clown; and the circus bandleader—blond, long-haired, miniskirted Mary Hartline. In addition to these regulars, each week guest jugglers, tumblers and animal acts were featured.

From left to right: ringmaster Claude Kirchner, bandleader Mary Hartline and Nick Francis of *Super Circus*, with a young member of the studio audience.

WCBS—TV Channel 2
WNBT Channel 4
WABD Channel 5
WATV Channel 13
WJZ—TV Channel 7
WOR—TV Channel 9
WPIX Channel 11

SUNDAY, SEPTEMBER 17

10:00-WNBT—Children's Theatre
10:10-WNBT—Film; Ace Drummond
10:30-WNBT—Children's Hour
11:30-WNBT—The Magic Clown
11:45-WNBT—Jon Gnagy Show
12:00-WNBT—News Review
12:15-WNBT—Who Said That?—Quiz
12:45-WNBT—U. N. Stamp Club
1:00-WATV—Junior Frolics
1:15-WOR-TV—Comedy Carnival
1:30-WOR-TV—Felton's Knothole Gang
2:00-WPIX—Larraine Day Show
WOR-TV—Baseball: Dodgers vs. Chicago, at Ebbets Field
2:25-WPIX—Baseball: St. Louis vs. Giants
2:30-WABD—Sunday Matinee (to 5:30)
2:45-WNBT—Singers of Israel: Cantor Samuel Malavsky and Family Choir
3:00-WATV—News; Feature Film
3:15-WNBT—Hanson Baldwin's Weekly War Room
3:30-WNBT—Zoo Parade
4:00-WNBT—Battle Report—Washington
WJZ-TV—Soap Box Theatre
WATV—Western Film
4:15-WCBS-TV—Music; Preview
4:30-WCBS-TV—Lamp Unto My Feet
WNBT—Meet the Press
WJZ-TV—Sunday at the Zoo
5:00-WCBS-TV—Capitol Cloak Room
WNBT—Watch the World, Current Events Show, With John Cameron Swayze
WJZ-TV—Super Circus
WOR-TV—Clubhouse Quiz
WPIX—Television Chapel
WATV—Junior Frolics
5:30-WCBS-TV—People's Platform: Should Germany Be Rearmed?—Brig. Gen. Frank Howley; James P. Warburg
WNBT—Film: Hopalong Cassidy
WPIX—Capt. Glenn's Bandwagon
WATV—Marie Moser Starlets
6:00-WCBS-TV—The Chuck Wagon
WJZ-TV—Cartoon Teletales
WATV—News; Feature Film
6:30-WCBS-TV—Mr. I: Imagination—Sketch, With Paul Tripp, Others
WNBT—Say It With Acting
WJZ-TV—Film: The Marshall Plan
WPIX—Newsreel
6:45-WPIX—Jimmy Powers—Sports
6:50-WABD—Time for Reflection
7:00-WCBS-TV—Gene Autry Show
WNBT—Leave It to the Girls: Joe Laurie Jr., Guest
WABD—Starlit Time, Variety
WJZ-TV—Think Fast—Quiz
WPIX—News—John Tillman
WATV—Western Film
7:15-WPIX—Voice of the People
7:30-WCBS-TV—This Is Show Business, With Clifton Fadiman, Abe Burrows, George S. Kaufman, Larraine Day, Jack Leonard, Bidu Sayao, Johnny Johnson
WNBT—The Aldrich Family—Comedy, With Dick Tyler, Jackie Kelk, Nancy Carroll, Others
WJZ-TV—Diane Doxee Show
8:00-WCBS-TV—Toast of the Town: Ed Sullivan, Hedy Lamarr, Pat O'Brien, Mimi Benzell, Others
WNBT—Comedy Hour: With Dean Martin and Jerry Lewis, Valerie Bettis, Marilyn Maxwell, Others
WABD—Rhythm Rodeo, With Art Jarrett
WJZ-TV—The Ruggles, Comedy
WATV—Feature Film
WPIX—Double Feature Theatre
8:30-WABD—Film Feature
WJZ-TV—Sit or Miss Game
WCBS-TV—Robert Q. Lewis Show
WNBT—Television Playhouse: The

Long Run, With Francis Lederer, Vickie Cummings
WABD—They Stand Accused
WJZ-TV—Stage Two, Revue
WATV—Western Film
9:15-WCBS-TV—Three's Company
9:30-WCBS-TV—Documentary: The Facts We Face
WJZ-TV—Faith for Today
10:00-WCBS-TV—John Daly, News; Brig. Gen. Frank Howley, Guest
WNBT—Garroway at Large
WABD—Yesterday's Newsreel
WJZ-TV—Film: The Marshall Plan
WPIX—Telenews Weekly
WATV—Feature Film
10:15-WCBS-TV—Film Theatre: Monster Maker, With J. Carroll Naish, Ralph Morgan, Wanda McKay
10:30-WNBT—To Be Announced
WPIX—Mayfair House Movies: A Star Is Born, With Janet Gaynor, Frederic March
11:00-WNBT—News Review of the Week
WATV—Feature Film
12:15-WPIX—Telepix News

MONDAY, SEPTEMBER 18

9:30-WNBT—Johnny Andrews Show
WABD—News, Ed Condit
9:45-WNBT—Josephine McCarthy, Cooking
WABD—Morning Chapel
10:00-WNBT—Kathi Norris Show
WABD—Baby Sitter—Pat Meikle
10:30-WABD—Kitchen Fare—Susan Adams
11:00-WNBT—Date in Manhattan
WABD—Television Shopper
11:30-WJZ-TV—The Fitzgeralds
11:45-WNBT—News Bob Wilson
12:00-WNBT—Carl Caruso
WABD—Headline Clues
WJZ-TV—Kitchen Kapers
WPIX—Music; Newsreel
12:30-WABD—Johnny Olsen Rumpus Room
WJZ-TV—Market Melodies
WPIX—Batter Up—Hal Tunis
12:45-WOR—Comedy Carnival
1:00-WNBT—News Summary
WABD—Okay Mother—Dennis James
WOR-TV—Felton's Knothole Gang
WPIX—Laraine Day Show
1:15-WCBS-TV—Facts and Forecasts
1:20-WPIX—Baseball: St. Louis vs. Giants, at Polo Grounds
1:25-WOR-TV—Baseball: Dodgers vs. Chicago, at Ebbets Field
1:30-WCBS-TV—About the House—Lydia Rogers, Woody Klose
WABD—Sidewalk Interviews
WATV—Home Economics—Ruth Bean
1:45-WABD—Susan Raye, Songs
2:00-WATV—Feature Film
2:30-WCBS-TV—The Real McKay
WJZ-TV—Telephone Game
3:00-WJZ-TV—Zeke Manners Show
WATV—Homemaker's Guide
3:30-WCBS-TV—Look Your Best, With Richard Willis
WNBT—Racing From Belmont Park
4:00-WCBS-TV—Homemakers' Exchange
WATV—Western Film
4:30-WCBS-TV—Vanity Fair
WOR-TV—Clubhouse Quiz
WPIX—Ted Steele Show
5:00-WCBS-TV—Lucky Pup
WNBT—NBC Comics
WJZ-TV—Mr. Magic
WATV—Junior Frolics
5:15-WCBS-TV—Life With Snarky Parker
WNBT—Panhandle Pete and Jennifer—Children's Show
WJZ-TV—Paddy Pelican
5:30-WCBS-TV—The Chuck Wagon
WNBT—Howdy Doody
WABD—Serial Theatre
WJZ-TV—Hold 'Er Newt
WPIX—Six Gun Playhouse
WATV—Feature Film
5:45-WJZ-TV—Space Patrol—Sketch
6:00-WNBT—Easy Does It—Variety
WABD—Small Fry Club
6:25-WNBT—News Don Goddard

6:30-WNBT—Tex and Jinx Interviews
WABD—Magic Cottage—Pat Meikle
WPIX—News; Weather
WATV—Texas Jim Robertson, Songs
6:45-WCBS-TV—Bob Howard Show
WPIX—Jimmy Powers
WATV—Western Short
6:55-WNET—Weather Man
7:00-WCBS-TV—Garry Moore Show
WNBT—Kukla, Fran and Ollie
WABD—Captain Video
WJZ-TV—News; Club Seven
WOR-TV—Camera on Korea
WPIX—News, John Tillman
WATV—Western Film
7:15-WPIX—Broadway Limited, With Dennis O'Keefe
7:30-WCBS-TV—Television News
WNBT—Roberta Quinlan Show
WABD—Manhattan Spotlight
WJZ-TV—Hollywood Screen Test
WOR-TV—Comedy Carnival
7:45-WCBS-TV—The Stork Club
WNBT—News Caravan
WABD—Hazel Scott, Songs
WOR-TV—Film: Riders of Destiny, With John Wayne
8:00-WCBS-TV—Pantomime Quiz
WNBT—Paul Winchell-Jerry Mahoney Show
WABD—Armed Forces Film
WJZ-TV—Treasury Men in Action
WATV—Feature Film
8:30-WCBS-TV—Godfrey's Talent Scouts
WNBT—Lily Pons, Soprano
WABD—Al Morgan Show
WJZ-TV—Author Meets the Critics
WPIX—To Be Announced
WATV—Finals of Miss Television, 1950, Contest
8:45-WOR-TV—Film: Accused, With Dolores Del Rio, Douglas Fairbanks Jr.
9:00-WCBS-TV—Candid Camera
WNBT—Lights Out: Leopard Lady, With Boris Karloff
WABD—Wrestling, Columbia Park
WJZ-TV—Double Feature Film
9:30-WCBS-TV—We Take Your Word
WNBT—To Be Announced
10:00-WCBS-TV—Studio One: Trilby, With Priscilla Gillette, Arnold Moss
10:15-WOR-TV—Top View in Sports
10:30-WNBT—Talent Search—Skitch Henderson
11:00-WCBS-TV—At Home Show: Earl Wrightson, Baritone
WNBT—Broadway Open House
WPIX—News; Weather; Sports
WATV—Star Dust Theatre
11:15-WCBS-TV—Allan Jackson, News
11:25-WCBS-TV—Midnight Snack, Variety
11:30-WPIX—Gail and Bill, Songs
11:45-WPIX—Night Owl Theatre
12:00-WATV—Western Short

TUESDAY, SEPTEMBER 19

9:30-WNBT—Johnny Andrews, Piano
WABD—News—Ed Condit
9:45-WNBT—Josephine McCarthy Show
WABD—Morning Chapel
10:00-WNBT—Kathi Norris Show
WABD—Baby Sitter
10:30-WABD—Kitchen Fare—Susan Adams
11:00-WNBT—Date in Manhattan
WABD—Television Shopper
11:30-WJZ-TV—The Fitzgeralds
11:45-WNBT—News-Bob Wilson
12:00-WNBT—Carl Caruso Program
WABD—Headline Clues
WJZ-TV—Kitchen Kapers
12:30-WABD—Johnny Olsen Rumpus Room
WJZ-TV—Market Melodies
WPIX—Batter Up—Hal Tunis
1:00-WNBT—News Summary
WABD—Okay, Mother—Dennis James
WOR-TV—Felton's Knothole Gang
WPIX—Laraine Day Program
1:15-WCBS-TV—Facts and Forecasts
1:20-WPIX—Baseball: Cincinnati vs. Giants, at Polo Grounds
1:25-WOR-TV—Baseball: Dodgers vs. Pittsburgh at Ebbets Field

1:30-WCBS-TV—About the House. With
Lydia Rogers. Woody Klose
WABD—Sidewalk interviews
WATV—Home Economics. Ruth Bean
1:45-WATV—Susan Raye. Songs
2:00-WATV—Feature Film
2:30-WCBS-TV—The Real McKay
WJZ-TV—Telephone Game
3:00-WCBS-TV, WNBT-U. N. General
Assembly. Flushing
WJZ-TV—Zeke Manners Show
WATV—Homemakers Guide
4:00-WCBS-TV—Homemakers' Exchange
WATV—Western Film
4:30-WCBS-TV—Vanity Fair
WPIX—Ted Steele Show
5:00-WCBS-TV—Lucky Pup
WNBT—NBC Comics
WJZ-TV—Mr. Magic
WATV—Junior Frolics
5:15-WCBS-TV—Life with Snarky Parker
WNBT—Panhandle Pete and Jennifer
—Children's Show
WJZ-TV—Paddy Pelican
5:30-WCBS-TV—The Chuck Wagon
WNBT—Howdy Doody
WABD—Serial Theatre
WJZ-TV—Hold 'er Newt
WPIX—Six-Gun Playhouse
WATV—Feature Film
5:45-WJZ-TV—Space Patrol—Sketch
6:00-WNBT—Easy Does It—Variety
WABD—Small Fry Club
6:25-WNBT—News; Don Goddard
6:30-WNBT—Tex and Jinx interviews
WABD—Magic Cottage—Pat Meikle
WOR-TV—Mystery Rider.
WPIX—News; Weather
WATV—Texas Jim Robertson. Songs
6:45-WCBS-TV—Bob Howard Show
WOR-TV—Time for Beany
WPIX—Jimmy Powers
WATV—Western Films
6:55-WNBT—Weather Man
7:00-WCBS-TV—Garry Moore Show
WNBT—Kukla, Fran and Ollie
WABD—Captain Video
WJZ-TV—News; Club Seven
WPIX—News—John Tillman
7:15-WOR-TV—Mr. and Mrs. Mystery
WPIX—Film: Scattergood Survives
a Murder. With Guy Kibbee
7:30-WCBS-TV—Television News
WNBT—John Conte Little Show
WABD—Eloise Salutes the Stars
WJZ-TV—Buster Keaton—Film
WOR-TV—Western Playhouse
7:45-WCBS-TV—Three's Company
WNBT—News Caravan
WABD—Joan Edwards Show
8:00-WCBS-TV—Sure as Fate: Run
From The Sun. With Robert Cum-
mings; Jean Gillespie
WNBT—Star Theatre, With Milton
Berle, Charles Coburn, Robert
Alda, Others
WABD—Court of Current Issues
WJZ-TV—Buck Rogers—Sketch
WOR-TV—Bowery Music Hall. With
Jack Linder
WATV—To Be Announced
8:30-WJZ-TV—Mysteries of Chinatown
WPIX—News; Sports
9:00-WCBS-TV—Winner Take All
WNBT—Fireside Theatre: Incident
in the Rain, With Irene Vernon,
Warren Douglass, Frances Williams
WABD—Cavalcade of Bands
WJZ-TV—Your Witness
WOR-TV—Wrestling From Bronx
Winter Garden
WPIX—To Be Announced
WATV—Stock Car Races
9:30-WCBS-TV—Suspense
WNBT—Circle Theatre: The Other
Woman. With Louise Albritton.
Glenn Langan
WJZ-TV—Motorboat Racing Film
10:00-WCBS-TV—Play: The Black Door,
With Dane Clark
WNBT—Amateur Hour—Ted Mack
WABD—Star Time With Frances
Langford, Benny Goodman, Lew
Parker; Others
WJZ-TV—Roller Derby
10:30-WCBS-TV—Red Barber's Clubhouse
10:45-WCBS-TV—Ned Calmer. Interviews
11:00-WCBS-TV—Alan Jackson, News

WNBT—Broadway Open House
WABD—Film: When Knights Were
Bold. With Jack Buchanan, Fay
Wray
WOR-TV—Starlit Playhouse
WPIX—News; Weather; Sports
WATV—Stardust Theatre
11:10-WCBS-TV—Midnight Snack. Variety
11:30-WPIX—Gail and Bill. Songs
11:45-WPIX—Night Owl Theatre
12:00-WATV—Western Short

WEDNESDAY, SEPTEMBER 20

9:30-WNBT—Johnny Andrews, Piano
WABD—News—Ed Condit
9:45-WNBT—Josephine McCarthy,
Cooking Show
WABD—Morning Chapel
10:00-WNBT—Kathi Norris Show
WABD—Baby Sitter
10:30-WABD—Kitchen Fare—Susan Adam
11:00-WNBT—Date in Manhattan
WABD—Television Shopper
11:30-WJZ-TV—The Fitzgeralds
11:45-WNBT—News—Bob Wilson
12:00-WNBT—Carl Caruso Program
WABD—Headline Clues
WJZ-TV—Kitchen Kapers
12:30-WABD—Johnny Olson Rumpus Room
WJZ-TV—Market Melodies
WPIX—Batter Up—Hal Tunis
1:00-WNBT—News Summary
WABD—Okay Mother—Dennis James
WOR-TV—Felton's Knothole Gang
WPIX—Laraine Day Show
1:15-WCBS-TV—Facts and Forecasts
1:20-WPIX—Baseball: Cincinnati vs.
Giants, at Polo Grounds
1:25-WOR-TV—Baseball: Dodgers vs.
Pittsburgh, at Ebbets Field
1:30-WCBS-TV—About the House. With
Lydia Rogers, Woody Klose
WABD—Sidewalk Interviews
WATV—Home Economics. Ruth Bean
1:45-WABD—Susan Raye, Songs
2:00-WATV—Feature Film
2:30-WCBS-TV—The Real McKay
WJZ-TV—Telephone Game
3:00-WJZ-TV—Zeke Manners Show
WATV—Homemakers Guide
3:30-WCBS-TV—Look Your Best. with
Richard Willis
WNBT—Racing from Aqueduct
4:00-WCBS-TV—Homemakers Exchange
WATV—Western Film
4:30-WCBS-TV—Vanity Fair
WOR-TV—Clubhouse Quiz—Bob Edge
WPIX—Ted Steele Show
5:00-WCBS-TV—Lucky Pup
WNBT—NBC Comics
WJZ-TV—Mr. Magic
WOR-TV—Starlit Matinee
WATV—Junior Frolics
5:15-WCBS-TV—Life With Snarky Parker
WNBT—Panhandle Pete and Jenni-
fer—Children's Show
WJZ-TV—Paddy Pelican
5:30-WCBS-TV—The Chuck Wagon
WNBT—Howdy Doody
WABD—Serial Theatre
WJZ-TV—Hold 'Er Newt
WPIX—Six Gun Playhouse
WATV—Feature Films
5:45-WJZ-TV—Space Patrol—Sketch
6:00-WNBT—Easy Does It. Variety
WABD—Small Fry Club
6:25-WNBT—News—Don Goddard
6:30-WNBT—Tex and Jinx Interviews
WABD—Magic Cottage—Pat Meikle
WOR-TV—Mystery Rider
WPIX—News; Weather
WATV—Texas Jim Robertson. Songs
6:45-WCBS-TV—Bob Howard Show
WOR-TV—Time for Beany
WPIX—Jimmy Powers
WATV—Western Short
6:55-WNBT—Weather—Tex Antoine
7:00-WCBS-TV—Jeanne Bargy Show
WNBT—Kukla, Fran and Ollie
WABD—Captain Video—Sketch
WJZ-TV—News; Club Seven
WOR-TV—Comedy Carnival
WPIX—News—John Tilman
WATV—Western News
7:15-WOR-TV—Mr. and Mrs. Mystery
WPIX—Film: Pack Up Your Troubles
7:30-WCBS-TV—Television News
WNBT—Roberta Quinlan

WABD—Manhattan Spotlight
WJZ-TV—Chance of a Lifetime.
With John Reed King
WOR-TV—Dinner at Sardi's
7:45-WCBS-TV—The Stork Club
WNBT—News Caravan
WABD—Hazel Scott. Songs
8:00-WCBS-TV—Gary Moore Show
WNBT—The Nature of Things
WABD—Film: Criminals Within
with Eric Linden. Ann Doran
WOR-TV—What's Offered?
WJZ-TV—On Trial
WATV—Feature Film
8:15-WNBT—Wendy Barrie Show
8:30-WNBT—Cameo Theatre: The Pa
Sack, with Dennis Harrison. Ga
Gordon, James Little
WJZ-TV—Film: Dick Tracy
WOR-TV—Tiny Fairbanks Show
WPIX—To Be Announced
8:45-WOR-TV—Today's News and Spo
9:00-WCBS-TV—Twine Time
WNBT—Television Theatre: L
Stop. with Mildred Dunnock. I
bel Price
WABD—Famous Jury Trials
WJZ-TV—Don McNeil TV Club
WOR-TV—Wrestling, Coney Island
Velodrome
WATV—Western Film
9:30-WCBS-TV—The Web: Murder's
Challenge
WABD—The Plainclothes Man—Pl
WPIX—Art Ford Show
10:00-WCBS-TV—Film: Shake Hands W
Murder, with Iris Adrian. Fra
Jenks, Douglas Fowley
WNBT—Break the Bank
WABD—Broadway to Hollywood
WJZ-TV—Wrestling, from Chicago
WATV—Broadway Theatre
10:30-WNBT—Stars Over Hollywood:
Girl or Ghost, with Gloria
Saunders
WABD—Yesterday's Newsreel
11:00-WCBS-TV—News—Allen Jackson
WNBT—Broadway Open House
WOR-TV—Starlit Playhouse
WPIX—News; Weather; Sports
WATV—Stardust Theatre
11:10-WCBS-TV—Midnight Snack. Varie
11:30-WPIX—Gail and Bill. Songs
11:45-WPIX—Night Owl Theatre
12:00-WATV—Western Short

THURSDAY, SEPTEMBER 21

9:30-WNBT—Johnny Andrews, Piano
WABD—News—Ed Condit
9:45-WNBT—Josephine McCarthy
Cooking Show
WABD—Morning Chapel
10:00-WNBT—Kathi Norris Show
WABD—Baby Sitter
10:30-WABD—Kitchen Fare—Susan Adar
11:00-WNBT—Date in Manhattan
WABD—Television Shopper
11:30-WJZ-TV—The Fitzgeralds
11:45-WNBT—News—Bob Wilson
12:00-WNBT—Carl Caruso Program
WABD—Headline Clues
WJZ-TV—Kitchen Kapers
12:30-WABD—Johnny Olsen Rumpus Roo
WJZ-TV—Market Melodies
WPIX—Batter Up—Hal Tunis
1:00-WNBT—News Summary
WABD—Okay Mother—Dennis Jame
WPIX—Laraine Day Show
WOR-TV—Felton's Knothole Gang
1:15-WCBS-TV—Facts and Forecasts
1:20-WPIX—Baseball: Cincinnati vs.
Giants. at Polo Grounds
1:25-WOR-TV—Baseball: Dodgers vs.
Pittsburgh, at Ebbets Field
1:30-WCBS-TV—About the House. Wit
Lydia Rogers, Woody Kluse
WABD—Susan Adams Kitchen
WATV—Home Economics—Ruth Bea
1:45-WABD—Susan Raye, Songs
2:00-WATV—Feature Film
2:30-WCBS-TV—The Real McKay
WJZ-TV—Telephone Game
3:00-WJZ-TV—Zeke Manners Show
WATV—Homemaker's Guide
4:00-WCBS-TV—Homemakers' Exchange
WATV—Western Film
4:30-WCBS-TV—Vanity Fair
WPIX—Ted Steele Show
WOR-TV—Clubhouse Quiz. Bob Edg

00-WCBS-TV—Lucky Pup
WNBT—NBC Comics
WJZ-TV—Mr. Magic
WATV—Junior Frolics
15-WCBS-TV—Life With Snarky Parker
WNBT—Panhandle Pete and Jennifer—Children's Show
WJZ-TV—Paddy Pelican
30-WCBS-TV—The Chuck Wagon
WNBT—Howdy Doody
WABD—Serial Theatre
WJZ-TV—Hold 'er Newt
WPIX—Six-Gun Playhouse
WATV—Feature Film
45-WJZ-TV—Space Patrol—Sketch
00-WNBT—Friendship Ranch—Variety
15-WNBT—Easy Does It—Variety
25-WNBT—News; Don Goddard
30-WNBT—Tex and Jinx—Interviews
WABD—Magic Cottage—Pat Meikle
WOR-TV—Mystery Rider
WPIX—News; Weather
WATV—Texas Jim Robertson, Songs
45-WCBS-TV—Bob Howard Show
WOR-TV—Time for Beany
WPIX—Jimmy Powers
WATV—Western Films
55-WNBT—The Weatherman
00-WCBS-TV—Garry Moore Show
WNBT—Kukla, Fran and Ollie
WABD—Captain Video
WJZ-TV—News; Club Seven
WOR-TV—Comedy Carnival
WPIX—News; Gail and Bill, Songs
15-WOR-TV—Mr. and Mrs. Mystery
WJZ-TV—Kiernan's Kaleidoscope
30-WCBS-TV—Television News
WNBT—John Conte's Little Show
WABD—Manhattan Spotlight
WJZ-TV—The Lone Ranger
WOR-TV—Let's Arbitrate
WPIX—Play—Leave It to Papa
45-WCBS-TV—Three's Company
WNBT—News Caravan
WABD—Joan Edwards, Songs
00-WCBS-TV—The Show Goes On
WNBT—Believe It or Not
WABD—Film: Mystery of the Thirteenth Guest, With Dick Purcell, Helen Parrish
WJZ-TV—Stop the Music
WOR-TV—Al Siegal's Music Shop
WPIX—Dixie Showboat
WATV—Stairway to Stardom
30-WNBT—Hawkins Falls
WOR-TV—News and Sports
WPIX—To Be Announced
45-WOR-TV—Boxing, Fort Hamilton
00-WCBS-TV—Alan Young Show; Jane Froman, Guest
WNBT—Jack Haley Show
WABD—Morey Amsterdam Show
WJZ-TV—Holiday Hotel—Comedy, With Don Ameche
WPIX—Wrestling—Ridgewood Grove
WATV—Western Film
30-WCBS-TV—Starlight Theatre
WABD—To Be Announced
WJZ-TV—Blind Date
00-WCBS-TV—Truth or Consequences
WNBT—Martin Kane, Private Eye—Play, With Bill Gargan
WJZ-TV—Roller Derby
WATV—Feature Film
30-WCBS-TV—Play: The Double Dyed Deceiver With Ian Keith, Ralph Rigg
WNBT—Quick on the Draw
00-WCBS-TV—Allen Jackson, News
WNBT—Broadway Open House
WOR-TV—Starlit Playhouse
WPIX—News; weather
WATV—Stardust Theatre
10-WJZ-TV—Midnight Snack, Variety
15-WJZ-TV—Red Grange Predicts
30-WPIX—Night Owl Theatre
30-WATV—Western Short

FRIDAY, SEPTEMBER 22
30-WNBT—Johnny Andrews, Piano
WABD—News—Ed Condit
45-WNBT—Josephine McCarthy
WABD—Morning Chapel
00-WNBT—Kathi Norris Show
WABD—Baby Sitter
30-WABD—Betsy Brewster's Kitchen
00-WNBT—Date in Manhattan
WABD—Television Shopper

11:30-WJZ-TV—The Fitzgeralds
11:45-WNBT—News—Bob Wilson
12:00-WNBT—Anne Pringle—Carl Caruso
WABD—Headline Clues
WJZ-TV—Kitchen Kapers
WPIX—Music; Newsreel
12:30-WABD—Johnny Olsen Rumpus Room
WJZ-TV—Market Melodies
12:45-WPIX—Matinee Movie
1:00-WNBT—News Summary
WABD—Okay Mother—Dennis James
WJZ-TV—Cooking—Dione Lucas
1:15-WCBS-TV—Facts and Forecasts
1:30-WCBS-TV—About the House, With Lydia Rogers, Woody Klose
WABD—Sidewalk Interviews
WJZ-TV—Market Melodies
WATV—Home Economics—Ruth Bean
1:45-WABD—Susan Raye, Songs
2:00-WATV—Feature Film
WPIX—Ted Steele Show
2:30-WCBS-TV—The Real McKay
WJZ-TV—Telephone Game
3:00-WJZ-TV—Zeke Manners Show
WATV—Homemakers' Guide
3:30-WCBS-TV—Look Your Best, with Richard Willis
4:00-WCBS-TV—Homemakers' Exchange
WATV—Feature Film
4:30-WCBS-TV—Vanity Fair
5:00-WCBS-TV—Lucky Pup
WNBT—NBC Comics
WJZ-TV—Mr. Magic
WPIX—News; Glenn's Bandwagon
WATV—Junior Frolics
5:15-WCBS-TV—Life With Snarky Parker
WNBT—Panhandle Pete and Jennifer—Children's Show
WJZ-TV—Paddy Pelican
5:30-WCBS-TV—The Chuck Wagon
WNBT—Howdy Doody
WABD—Serial Theatre
WJZ-TV—Hold 'er Newt
WPIX—Six Gun Playhouse
WATV—Feature Film
5:45-WJZ-TV—Space Patrol—Sketch
6:00-WNBT—Easy Does It—Variety
WABD—Small Fry Club
6:25-WNBT—News—Don Goddard
6:30-WNBT—Tex and Jinx—Interviews
WABD—Magic Cottage—Pat Meikle
WOR-TV—The Mystery Rider
WPIX—News; Weather
WATV—Texas Jim Robertson, Songs
6:45-WCBS-TV—Bob Howard Show
WOR-TV—Time for Beany
WPIX—Jimmy Powers
WATV—Weather Films
6:55-WNBT—Weatherman—Tex Antoine
7:00-WCBS-TV—Garry Moore Show
WNBT—Kukla, Fran and Ollie
WABD—Captain Video
WJZ-TV—News; Club Seven
WOR-TV—Comedy Carnival
WPIX—News—John Tillman
7:15-WOR-TV—Mr. and Mrs. Mystery
WPIX—Film: It Happened in New Orleans, With Benita Hume
7:30-WCBS-TV—Television News
WNBT—Roberta Quinlan Show
WABD—Manhattan Spotlight
WJZ-TV—Corrigan's Ranch, Variety
WOR-TV—Bobby Benson—Sketch
7:45-WCBS-TV—The Stork Club
WNBT—News Caravan
WABD—Hazel Scott, Songs
8:00-WCBS-TV—Mama, With Peggy Wood
WNBT—The Quiz Kids
WABD—To Be Announced
WJZ-TV—My True Story
WOR-TV—Twenty Questions
WATV—News; Film Short
8:30-WCBS-TV—Detective's Wife—Play, With Lynn Bari, Donald Curtis
WNBT—We, the People
WABD—Hold That Camera
WJZ-TV—Football Giants Huddle
WOR-TV—Play: Trapped
WPIX—Football: Boston College vs. Wake Forest, at Braves Field, Boston
8:35-WATV—Wrestling Matches, From Meadowbrook Bowl
9:00-WCBS-TV—Theatre Hour: The Married Look, With Paul Kelly
WNBT—Versatile Varieties
WABD—Hands of Mystery
WOR-TV—Library of Art Films

WOR-TV—Wrestling, Jamaica Arena
9:30-WNBT—The Clock: The Morning After, With Raymond Massey, Mady Christians
WABD—Roscoe Karns, Inside Detective—Sketch
WJZ-TV—Tin Pan Alley TV
10:00-WCBS-TV—Star of the Family, With Morton Downey
WNBT—Boxing: Madison Square Garden
WABD—Cavalcade of Stars
WJZ-TV—Penthouse Party
10:30-WCBS-TV—By Popular Demand, With Arlene Francis
WJZ-TV—Mystery Film
10:45-WNBT—Fights of the Century
11:00-WCBS-TV—Alan Dale Show
WNBT—Broadway Open House
WABD—John Feeney Show
WOR-TV—Starlit Playhouse
WPIX—News; Weather; Sports
WATV—Stardust Theatre
11:30-WCBS-TV—Allan Jackson, News
WPIX—Gail and Bill, Songs
11:40-WJZ-TV—Midnight Snack, Variety
11:45-WPIX—Night Owl Theatre
12:00-WATV—Western Short

SATURDAY, SEPTEMBER 23
11:00 A. M.-WJZ-TV—Saturday at the Zoo
11:30-WJZ-TV—Acrobat Ranch
12:00-WJZ-TV—Animal Clinic
WPIX—Music; Newsreel
12:45-WPIX—Matinee Movie
1:00-WATV—Of Human Interest
1:45-WABD—Dizzy Dean
1:55-WABD—Baseball: Yankees vs. Boston, at Yankee Stadium
2:00-WPIX—Ted Steele Show
2:30-WPIX—Football: Yale vs. Connecticut, at New Haven
3:00-WATV—Feature Film
3:30-WNBT—Horse Racing, Aqueduct
4:00-WATV—Western Film
4:30-WABD—Dizzy Dean
5:00-WOR-TV—Italian Feature Film
WPIX—News; Glenn's Bandwagon
WATV—Junior Frolics
5:30-WNBT—Joe DiMaggio Show
WPIX—Six Gun Playhouse
5:45-WNBT—To Be Announced
6:00-WABD—Frontier Theatre: Lion's Den, With Tim McCoy
WATV—Feature Film
6:15-WCBS-TV—Week in Review
6:30-WCBS-TV—Lucky Pup
WNBT—Smilin' Ed McConnell and His Gang
WOR-TV—Mystery Rider
WPIX—Sports Telecade; Films
6:45-WOR-TV—Time for Beany
WPIX—Jimmy Powers
7:00-WCBS-TV—The Big Top
WNBT—Hank McCune Show
WABD—Captain Video
WOR-TV—Comedy Carnival
WPIX—News; John Tillman
WATV—Western Film
7:15-WOR-TV—Mr. and Mrs. Mystery
WPIX—Film: Oliver Twist
7:30-WCBS-TV—One Man's Family—Drama
WABD—Film: Woman in the Hall, With Ursula Jean, Jean Simmons
WJZ-TV—Film: Marshal of Gunsight Pass
WOR-TV—Talent Parade
8:00-WCBS-TV—Beat the Clock
WNBT—Saturday Night Revue: Jack Carter Show
WJZ-TV—Paul Whiteman, Teen Club
WATV—Your Congressman
8:30-WOR-TV—Today's News and Sports
WPIX—To Be Announced
WATV—Stock Car Races
8:45-WOR-TV—Johnny Farrell Golf Club
9:00-WCBS-TV—Premiere Playhouse
WNBT—Sid Caesar-Imogene Coca
WABD—Country Style, Variety
WJZ-TV—Roller Derby
WPIX—Boxing, Ridgewood Grove
10:00-WABD—Wrestling From Chicago
10:30-WNBT—To Be Announced
11:00-WOR-TV—Starlit Playhouse
WPIX—News; Weather, Music
WATV—Stardust Theatre
11:30-WPIX—Night Owl Theatre

WNBT CHANNEL 4

THE NEW YORK TIMES, SUNDAY, SEPTEMBER 17, 1950.

a strapping singer and a startling gad-fly

DEAN MARTIN & JERRY LEWIS

starring in a great revue

COLGATE COMEDY HOUR

. . . .

and great viewing all night long

4:30 Meet The Press	**8:00** Colgate Comedy Hour
5:00 Watch The World	**9:00** Philco Television Playhouse presents THE LONG RUN starring Francis Lederer
5:30 Hopalong Cassidy	
6:30 Say It With Acting	
7:00 Leave It To The Girls	**10:00** Garroway At Large
7:30 Aldrich Family	**10:30** This Week's News in Review

1950

NORTH KOREAN COMMUNISTS IN-
VADE SOUTH . . . . TRUMAN ORDERS
MACARTHUR TO KOREA . . . . UNITED
NATIONS FORMS ARMY TO REPEL COM-
MUNIST INVASION OF SOUTH KOREA
. . . . FORMOSA NEUTRALIZED BY U.S.
7TH FLEET . . . . CHINESE COMMUNISTS
INVADE SOUTH KOREA . . . . MAC-
ARTHUR CROSSES 38TH PARALLEL IN-
TO NORTH KOREA . . . . CHINESE DRIVE
UN FORCES BELOW 38TH . . . .

WHAT'S MY LINE?

The granddaddy of all TV quiz panel shows, *What's My Line?*, made its television debut on February 2, 1950, with columnist Dorothy Kilgallen, actress Arlene Francis and humorist Hal Block and Louis Untermeyer constituting the panel that tried to guess the occupations of contestants. John Daly was the show's moderator and host. Sunday night on CBS was *What's My Lines'*? permanent address for almost twenty years. When Block and Untermeyer left the show, they were replaced by Bennett Cerf and Fred Allen, whose slot was filled by Steve Allen after his death. Cerf and the Misses Kilgallen and Francis were permanent panelists the majority of years the show was on network TV. The producing team of Goodson and Todman, who also produced most of television's other panel shows, syndicated their *What's My Line?* program after CBS canceled the long-running show.

What's My Line? panelists Bennett Cerf, Arlene Francis, Dorothy Kilgallen and Fred Allen with moderator John Daly.

JACK BENNY

By 1950 the handwriting was on the wall as far as radio broadcasting was concerned, and many of that medium's stars were somewhat reluctantly making their moves to TV. Jack Benny, one of radio's brightest stars, made his TV debut in October, 1950, bringing with him most of his popular radio cast. Rochester (Eddie Anderson), announcer Don Wilson, vocalist Dennis Day and Jack's wife, Mary Livingston (who was less enthusiastic about TV than radio) all turned up. Benny's TV show was more variety than situation comedy, and Jack concentrated on introducing show-business celebrities from the movies and radio to TV audiences. Actress Marilyn Monroe and singer Johnny Ray were just two of the stars who made their TV debuts on *The Jack Benny Show*. In 1960 Jack decided to drop the weekly TV grind and has since concentrated on specials and occasional guest appearances.

On Jack Benny's first TV show, he appeared as a violin-playing hillbilly, to the delight of his watching audience.

YOU BET YOUR LIFE

You Bet Your Life star Groucho and his famed duck.

Groucho Marx deserted famed brothers Harpo and Chico when, in 1950, he became the star of his own weekly television series, *You Bet Your Life*. The show, a comedy-quiz program, had remarkable staying power on TV considering its simple format. With his announcer, George Fenneman, who was often the butt of Groucho's caustic remarks, cigar-puffing, bushy-mustached Groucho asked contestants impossible questions. Should they say the "secret word," a strange-looking duck would appear with a beakful of money. The show remained on the air well into the sixties.

Announcer George Fenneman and Groucho.

GARRY MOORE SHOW

A popular daytime variety show was MC'd by former Jimmy Durante sidekick Garry Moore and presented by CBS in 1950. Denise Lor, Ken Carson and Durward Kirby were regulars on the show, which remained on the air until 1958. That year, Moore became the star of a nighttime series—a weekly hour-long variety-music show which featured comediennes Marion Lorne and Carol Burnett, as well as old standby Durward Kirby. When the sensational Miss Burnett left the show in the mid-1960's, it lost much of its luster, and Garry retired from television for several years to rest and recuperate from the grueling weekly TV grind. He has since returned to television as MC of a syndicated quiz show and can also be seen as a guest star on

Moore's 1958 nighttime variety show comes to a close. Seen left to right, regulars Marion Lorne and Durward Kirby, guest Mahalia Jackson, Garry, guests Marge and Gower Champion and regular Carol Burnett.

such shows as Miss Burnett's own weekly comedy series.

Garry Moore's 1950 daytime show featured musical director Howard Smith, announcer Durward Kirby, Garry, singers Denise Lor and Ken Carson.

THE KATE SMITH HOUR

Early-afternoon television was graced in 1950 by the presence of Miss Kate Smith. NBC brought the former leading light of radio before TV cameras in a combination chatter, interview and song show, directed to the ladies of the house. Kate's longtime manager and friend, Ted Collins, was on hand with Kate, and an impressive list of guest stars from the world of show business appeared on the program. Miss Smith's TV popularity was such that NBC rewarded her with an evening musical-variety show, which ran in conjunction with the daytime show. Since 1954, when Kate's shows left the air, she has been seen regularly as a guest star on most of television's leading comedy-variety programs.

Ted Collins and Kate Smith are seen with Jeff Clark, one of the many guests on *The Kate Smith Hour.*

BURNS AND ALLEN

Radio stars George Burns and Gracie Allen, a celebrated husband and wife comedy team who had begun their careers as vaudeville performers in the 1920's, brought their famous routines to television in 1950, in a weekly situation comedy series on CBS. Cast regulars, Bea Benadaret as next door neighbor Blanche Norton, Larry Keaton as Blanche's husband, Harry, announcer Harry Von Zell and the Burnses' son, Ronny, were on hand to add to the comedy of the program. Gracie left the show because of ill health in 1958, and one year later the show retired from the air. Few viewers will forget the gruff, lovable George and his cigar-smoking monologues, which were mostly about Gracie, the muddleheaded queen with a strange kind of logic all her own.

George Burns and Gracie Allen

COLGATE COMEDY HOUR

The Colgate Comedy Hour, first seen in 1950, presented some of the biggest names in show business as hosts on an alternating basis. Some of the notables to serve in this capacity were Dean Martin and Jerry Lewis, Fred Allen, Eddie Cantor, Jimmy Durante, Abbott and Costello, Spike Jones and his City Slickers and Bob Hope. The list of guest stars who also appeared on this series included Martha Raye, Tennessee Ernie Ford, Jack Carter and Perry Como. Every now and then a special full-length musical comedy was presented. Musical comedy star Ethel Merman appeared in a special telecast of *Anything Goes*, and Bobby Clark was seen in *The Would-be Gentleman*. Other special attractions of the *Comedy Hour* included a presentation of *Ice Capades of 1954* with Donna Atwood.

Elaine May and Mike Nichols were featured on the *Comedy Hour* before both went their separate ways to become leading writers and directors.

Jerry Lewis and Dean Martin were *Colgate Comedy Hour* hosts.

THE ROY ROGERS SHOW

Cowboy star Roy Rogers, accompanied by his wife, Dale Evans, his horse, Trigger, and his dog, Bullet, also arrived on the television scene in 1950. His show, a combination song-fest and adventure series proved popular with the small fry and enjoyed a long, successful TV stay.

Roy Rogers, his horse, Trigger, and his wife, Dale Evans, in the syndicated *Roy Rogers Show.*

ROOTIE KAZOOTIE

Hand puppet Rootie Kazootie, his baseball cap tipped to one side, and his pal, Todd Russell, entertained kids daily on NBC, beginning in October, 1950. The young viewers squealed with delight each time puppets El Squeeko Mouse, Gala Poochie and Polka Dottie put in their appearances on the show. Order was preserved in between movie cartoons by the Keystone Kops. The show lasted until November, 1952.

Host Todd Russell, Rootie Kazootie, Gala Poochie, Polka Dottie and a Keystone Kop of *The Rootie Kazootie Show.*

BROADWAY OPEN HOUSE

During the early 1950's one of the most popular late-night comedy-talk shows was *Broadway Open House*. It starred comedian Jerry Lester and featured a tall, curvaceous blonde with the suitably Scandinavian name of Dagmar. The forerunner of NBC's current late-night offering, *The Tonight Show*, Lester's late-late opus with its Beanbag Club and hilarious takeoffs of fairy tales, which featured big Dagmar as such unlikely characters as Little Red Riding Hood and Little Miss Muffet, convulsed audiences. Other regulars on the show included David Street, Wayne Howell and musical director and accordionist Milton Delugg.

Broadway Open House star **Jerry Lester is surrounded by regulars on the show.**

THE FRANK SINATRA SHOW

Singing star Frank Sinatra made his TV debut in a weekly half hour musical program on CBS in 1950. It ran for two years. Since 1952 Frank has turned to special shows and guest spots, appearing on *The Colgate Comedy Hour,* with Bing Crosby, and *The Chevy Show* with Dinah Shore.

Frank Sinatra, the star of his own show in 1952.

ARTHUR MURRAY'S DANCE PARTY

A popular program which was publicly recalled each time one network or another canceled it was *The Arthur Murray Dance Party*, which first appeared in 1950. Originally designed to give on-the-air dance instructions to at-home viewers (à la the Arthur Murray Dance Studios), a musical-variety show format eventually evolved. Kathryn Murray, Arthur's energetic and vivacious wife, was the real star of the show, with Arthur doing his duty as a straight man or dance partner. The Murrays managed to squeeze a nine-year run out of the series before retiring to Hawaii.

Kathryn and Arthur Murray.

YOUR HIT PARADE

In 1950 NBC dusted off its old *Hit Parade* radio show, which had been such a hit in the 1940's, and moved it to television as a summer replacement. By October sufficient public interest had been aroused to keep the show on as a permanent attraction. Eileen Wilson, Snooky Lanson and Dorothy Collins were the singing stars, and Raymond Scott provided the musical background. In 1952 June Valli replaced Miss Wilson, and Russell Arms joined her, Miss Collins and Mr. Lanson. Gisele MacKenzie replaced Miss Valli the following season. But by 1958 it was clear that rock-and-roll music was going to dominate the song popularity charts for a long time to come. Highly stylized, the songs were almost inseparable from the artists who made them famous. Since the "Hit Paraders" were not familiar with that kind of music and since some of the hit tunes remained in the top ten for weeks on end, novel ways of staging the songs became more difficult. In 1959 the "Lucky Strike Gang" swayed back and forth singing "So long for a while . . . that's all the songs for a while" for the last time.

Russell Arms (standing second from left), June Valli, Snooky Lanson, Dorothy Collins and Raymond Scott and the Lucky Strike Hit Parade Chorus sing "So long for a while . . . "

BEAT THE CLOCK

Once a week Bud Collyer led studio contestants through some pretty exhausting paces as they tried to beat the clock by performing close to impossible stunts. Mr. Collyer's beautiful blond assistant, Roxanne, who introduced the contestants to Mr. Collyer and the home viewers, became a TV celebrity in her own right.

MC Bud Collyer of *Beat the Clock.*

BIG TOP

The Big Top, a popular CBS circus show, made its television debut in 1950, with ringmaster Jack Sterling presiding. Clowns, high-wire acts and animals, as well as interviews with kids in the studio audience, were featured weekly. Mr. Sterling was assisted by clown Ed McMahon, who later became better known as Johnny Carson's *Tonight Show* sidekick. The program had a healthy seven-year run on CBS before blowing its circus whistle for the last time in September, 1957.

Ringmaster Jack Sterling and clown Ed McMahon of CBS' *The Big Top.*

BOB HOPE

Bob Hope's annual Christmas show with the boys overseas has been a TV ritual. He is seen here with Maria "The Body" McDonald during one of these shows.

America's favorite comedian.

America's favorite comedian, Bob Hope, made his television debut on *The Star Spangled Revue*, on NBC, in 1950. He's been seen regularly on TV ever since. He has starred in such shows as *The Chesterfield Sound-Off Time, The Colgate Comedy Hour* and a monthly *Bob Hope Show*. His Christmas shows with servicemen and women overseas and his Academy Award presentation appearances have been annual musts for millions of TV viewers.

The star of the legitimate theater's successful *Blackout* shows, Ken Murray had a CBS television show of his own from 1950 to 1952. A veteran showman and vaudevillian, Murray was one of the first performers to realize TV's potential for keeping vaudeville alive. His variety extravaganzas proved just the right thing to revive this dying form of entertainment. Ken's sidekick, a pretty, wide-eyed cowgirl named Laurie Anders, added to the *Murray Show* merriment.

Ken Murray and Laurie Anders.

SUPERMAN

"It's a bird ... it's a plane ... *it's Superman! The Adventures of Superman* enjoyed the same success on television it had in comic strips, on the radio and in motion pictures. George Reeves played the dual role of Clark Kent and Superman. Noel Neill was seen as Lois Lane, Jack Larson played teen-aged copyboy Jimmy, and John Hamilton *Daily Planet* newspaper editor in chief Perry White. The show first appeared on TV screens across the country as a syndicated series in 1950 and has been shown continuously ever since.

George Reeves as *Superman.*

1951

MACARTHUR RELIEVED OF KOREAN COMMAND AFTER DEMANDING INVASION OF RED CHINA . . . . ARMISTICE TALKS BETWEEN UN AND KOREAN COMMUNISTS BEGIN AT PANMUNJON . . . . JAPANESE PEACE TREATY SIGNED BY 49 NATIONS IN SAN FRANCISCO . . . . ALGER HISS GOES TO PRISON FOR PERJURY . . . .

ABBOTT AND COSTELLO

Bud Abbott and Lou Costello.

The comedy team of Bud Abbott and Lou Costello had a situation comedy series in the early 1950's after making several guest appearances on *The Colgate Comedy Hour*. The series, which featured variations of their "Who's on first?" comedy routine, also starred actress Hillary Brooke.

AMAHL AND THE NIGHT VISITORS

The Three Kings, played by Leon Lishner, Andrew McKinley and David Aiken, and Amahl's mother, played by Rosemary Kuhlman, in a scene from *Amahl and the Night Visitors*.

The first opera commissioned expressly for television, Gian Carlo Menotti's *Amahl and the Night Visitors*, was premiered on Christmas Eve, 1951. In this story of a crippled boy who plays host to the Three Kings on their way to pay tribute to the Christ Child in Bethlehem, Chet Allen appeared as the boy, Amahl, and Rosemary Kuhlman sang the role of his mother. Response to the show was so great that NBC made the opera an annual Christmas tradition.

THE ERNIE KOVACS SHOW

Comic genius Ernie Kovacs.

The bizarre, wildly original, zany comic talents of comedian Ernie Kovacs first began delighting TV audiences in 1951, when his show was televised from Philadelphia over the NBC national network. Ernie was the first comedian to realize the unique potentials TV held for comedians. His close-up direct conversations with the camera, his special camera effects, his Nairobi tribe of music-playing gorillas had audiences howling. And who could forget his Percy Dovetonsils, the nasal-sounding poet with eyeglasses as thick as a soda pop bottle? In 1955 Ernie's show included his wife, Edie Adams, who did brilliant takeoffs on actresses Marilyn Monroe and Zsa Zsa Gabor. Ernie's show was canceled in 1956, and thereafter he confined his television activities to occasional guest appearances and specials such as *Ernie in Kovacsland*. His career was cut tragically short when he was killed in an auto accident in 1962. His unique TV comic spirit has never been equaled.

Pianist Eddie Hatrak with Edie Adams and Ernie.

Zany Lucy cuts up with a more sober Desi Arnaz.

The Ricardos and the Mertzes found themselves in jail in this *I Lovy Lucy* episode. From left to right: guest Will Wright, Ricky (Desi), Ethel, Lucy, Fred, and Tennessee Ernie Ford.

I LOVE LUCY

The most successful situation comedy series in the history of television, *I Love Lucy*, starring Lucille Ball and Desi Arnaz, first saw the glow of TV success in 1951. The show revolved around bandleader Ricky Ricardo (Arnaz), his zany, trouble-prone wife, Lucy (Miss Ball), and their funny neighbors and friends Fred and Ethel Mertz, played by William Frawley and Vivian Vance. Loosely based on Miss Ball's hit radio show *My Favorite Husband* and retaining many of her original writers, the *Lucy* show quickly became a national institution. In 1952, when Miss Ball became pregnant, zealous TV officials decided to make Lucy Ricardo pregnant as well.

The birth of Lucy's TV baby, a boy who was called Little Ricky, made

Lucy Ball awaits the birth of her celebrated baby.

national headlines. In real life Miss Ball had had a baby girl. Following his divorce from Miss Ball, Mr. Arnaz retired from the series. The following year Lucy returned alone with a new format and show titled *The Lucille Ball Show*. During *I Love Lucy*'s heyday the Desilu Company initiated a one-hour dramatic series called *The Desilu Playhouse*, which also had a profitable run on TV.

Fred and Ethel Mertz were played by Vivian Vance and William Frawley.

THE SENATE CRIME HEARINGS

In March, 1951, television came into its own with in-depth, on-the-spot coverage of important news events. CBS and NBC simultaneously presented the U.S. Senate hearings on crime in America. All day long, viewers would sit fascinated in front of their TV sets as Senators Estes Kefauver and Charles Tobey and lawyer Rudolph Halley questioned such czars of the underworld as Frank Costello and ex-gangsters' moll Virginia Hill. Most of the witnesses pleaded the Fifth—"I refuse to answer on the grounds that it may tend to incriminate me"—a statement that became a household phrase in homes all over America. Because of the hearings, Americans were made frighteningly aware of how a national web of crime could touch their everyday lives.

AMOS 'N' ANDY

Amos, Andy, the Kingfish, Sapphire and all the funny folk of the popular *Amos 'n' Andy* radio show were transferred to television in 1951 with an all-black cast. The characters of Amos and Andy, originally played on radio by white actors Charles Correll and Freeman Gosden, were portrayed on TV by Spencer Williams (Andy) and Alvin Childress (Amos). The most popular character on the program remained the Kingfish, played by Tim Moore. The show was finally canceled from television in 1953, when the NAACP and other civil-rights groups protested the way the show pictured the American black man.

Spencer Williams and Alvin Childress as Amos and Andy.

JACKIE GLEASON

Jackie Gleason's first television show was called *The Cavalcade of Stars* and was broadcast over the New York local Dumont station. The program featured all of Jackie's famous TV characters—the Poor Soul, Reggie Van Gleason, Ralph Cramden and Joe the Bartender. Also appearing on the show were comedienne Pert Kelton and comic Larry Storch. In 1952 Gleason's national drawing power was put to the test. He gained instant fame across the country as star of a network variety-comedy series. One of the popular features of the Gleason show, the Honeymooners, proved so popular that a separate half hour situation comedy series was created from it.

"And away we go!"—Gleason's famous line.

"The Honeymooners"—Ralph Cramden (Gleason), his neighbor Ed Norton (Art Carney), his wife, Alice (Audrey Meadows), and Ed's wife, Trixie (Joyce Randolph).

The Goodyear Playhouse's A Visit to a Small Planet, presented in 1955, featured Louis Edmonds, Cyril Ritchard and Jill Kraft.

A successful motion picture was made of *The Catered Affair*, first seen on *The Goodyear Playhouse* in 1955. Thelma Ritter and Pat Henning starred in the television version of the play.

THE GOODYEAR PLAYHOUSE

Lillian Gish and Eva Marie Saint starred in *A Trip to Bountiful,* in 1953.

The Goodyear Playhouse dramatic series, produced by Fred Coe, was responsible for bringing some of television's most successful and celebrated plays before the public. Paddy Chayefsky's award-winning *Marty*, starring Rod Steiger in the title role, later would win an Academy Award for Ernest Borgnine when it was made into a major motion picture. *The Catered Affair*, with Thelma Ritter, was also made into a motion picture starring Bette Davis, and *The Bachelor Party* became yet another successful film. *The Goodyear Playhouse* was also the first to present *A Trip to Bountiful*, with Lillian Gish, and Gore Vidal's *A Visit to a Small Planet*, both of which were later made into Broadway stage plays. In 1957 the series became a half hour show and closed its curtain for the final time a short time later.

PINKY LEE SHOW

Lisping burlesque comedian Pinky Lee first appeared in the weekly musical-variety series *The Two of Us* with Vivian Blaine in 1951. The show ran for two years on NBC. In 1953 Pinky brought his baggy suit and funny hat to daytime TV, with a show designed for the kiddies. During one of these shows Pinky, while still "on the air," collapsed and thereafter retired from TV.

The Two of Us **starred Vivian Blaine and Pinky Lee.**

RACKET SQUAD

One weekly TV mystery-crime show which provided a public service, as well as entertainment, was CBS' *Racket Squad*. The series, which starred Reed Hadley as Detective Braddock of the Racket Squad, informed viewers of the workings of various confidence-game racketeers, alerting viewers to beware of charming strangers. Captain Braddock arrested his last con man in 1953, but the show can still be seen on local reruns.

Reed Hadley as Captain Braddock of *Racket Squad.*

MACY'S THANKSGIVING DAY PARADE

Thanksgiving just wouldn't be the same without a telecast of *Macy's Annual Thanksgiving Day Parade*. The huge balloons of Mickey Mouse, Popeye the Sailor Man and other well known cartoon characters have been ushering in the Christmas shopping season for television viewers since 1951. Such notable TV personalities as Arlene Francis, Dave Garroway, Douglas Edwards, Bess Myerson and Marilyn Van Derbur have acted as TV hosts for the *Parade* over the years.

Guest star Frank Sinatra and Dinah Shore of *The Chevy Show.*

KUKLA, FRAN AND OLLIE

One puppet TV show, which was probably enjoyed by as many adults as children was NBC's *Kukla, Fran and Ollie* show. Actress Fran Allison's conversations with Burr Tillstrom's cloth and plaster characters had everyone believing the puppets were flesh and blood. First seen on local television in Chicago in 1947, it became a national network show in 1949.

Gentle Kukla, with his high voice and round, bulbous nose; lovable Ollie the Dragon, with his good-natured conceit; busty, overbearing Madame Oglepuss; cantankerous Beulah the Witch; "Dumb" Cecil Bill and his "Do-De-Doi-Doi;" Windbag Colonel Crackie; Dolores Dragon, Ollie's niece; Mercedes and Fletcher

The Kuklapolitan Players, from left to right, Colonel Crackie, Cecil Bill, Mercedes, Kukla, Ollie, Madame Oglepuss, Beulah the Witch and Fletcher Rabbitt.

Rabbitt, all controlled and spoken for by master puppeteer Mr. Tillstrom, won a permanent place for themselves in the hearts of millions of Americans. One of the show's most popular features was the performances of plays and operettas by the Kuklapolitan Players, which included all the puppets and Miss Allison. When *Kukla, Fran and Ollie* was dropped in 1954, public demand for its return was so strong NBC brought back the show for another five years. Since 1957 Mr. Tillstrom and his puppets have been seen as guests on various variety shows and specials and can be seen on NET-TV. This show remains in the memories of the public as one of the classics of TV's Golden Age.

MR. I. MAGINATION

Each weekday young television fans paid a visit to *Mr. I. Magination*'s "Imagination Town." From April, 1949, to June, 1952, youngsters could have "their every wish come true" in this magical town, created just for them by Mr. I. Magination himself, Paul Tripp. Stories, games, songs and crafts were the daily order of business in Imagination Town.

Mr. I. Magination—Paul Tripp.

SUPER CIRCUS

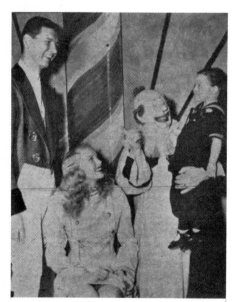

A very popular show for kids was *Super Circus*, which was presented by ABC from 1949 to 1956. The regular circus troupe that appeared on the show included ringmaster Claude Kirchner; clowns Cliffy, the tramp, Scampy, the boy clown, and Nick Francis, the fat clown; and the circus bandleader—blond, long-haired, mini-skirted Mary Hartline. In addition to these regulars, each week guest jugglers, tumblers and animal acts were featured.

From left to right: ringmaster Claude Kirchner, bandleader Mary Hartline and Nick Francis of *Super Circus*, with a young member of the studio audience.

WCBS—TV	Channel 2	WJZ—TV	Channel 7
WNBT	Channel 4	WOR—TV	Channel 9
WABD	Channel 5	WPIX	Channel 11
WATV	Channel 13		

SUNDAY, SEPTEMBER 17

:00-WNBT—Children's Theatre
:10-WNBT—Film: Ace Drummond
:30-WNBT—Children's Hour
:30-WNBT—The Magic Clown
:45-WNBT—Jon Gnagy Show
:00-WNBT—News Review
:15-WNBT—Who Said That?—Quiz
:45-WNBT—U. N. Stamp Club
:00-WATV—Junior Frolics
:15-WOR-TV—Comedy Carnival
:30-WOR-TV—Felton's Knothole Gang
:00-WPIX—Larraine Day Show
  WOR-TV—Baseball: Dodgers vs.
    Chicago, at Ebbets Field
:25-WPIX—Baseball: St. Louis vs. Giants
:30-WABD—Sunday Matinee (to 5:30)
:45-WNBT—Singers of Israel: Cantor
    Samuel Malavsky and Family
    Choir
:00-WATV—News: Feature Film
:15-WNBT—Hanson Baldwin's Weekly
    War Room
:30-WNBT—Zoo Parade
:00-WNBT-Battle Report—Washington
  WJZ-TV—Soap Box Theatre
  WATV—Western Film
:15-WCBS-TV—Music: Preview
:30-WNBT—Lamp Unto My Feet
  WNBT—Meet the Press
  WJZ-TV—Sunday at the Zoo
:00-WCBS-TV—Capitol Cloak Room
  WNBT—Watch the World. Current
    Events Show, With John Cameron
    Swayze
  WJZ-TV—Super Circus
  WOR-TV—Clubhouse Quiz
  WPIX—Television Chapel
  WATV—Junior Frolics
:30-WCBS-TV—People's Platform:
    Should Germany Be Rearmed?—
    Brig. Gen. Frank Howley; James
    P. Warburg
  WNBT—Film: Hopalong Cassidy
  WPIX—Capt. Glenn's Bandwagon
  WATV—Marie Moser Starlets
:00-WCBS-TV—The Chuck Wagon
  WJZ-TV—Cartoon Teletales
  WATV—News: Feature Film
:30-WCBS-TV—Mr. I: Magination—
    Sketch, With Paul Tripp, Others
  WNBT—Say It With Acting
  WJZ-TV—Film: The Marshall Plan
  WPIX—Newsreel
:45-WPIX—Jimmy Powers—Sports
:59-WABD—Time for Reflection
:00-WCBS-TV—Gene Autry Show
  WNBT—Leave It to the Girls: Joe
    Laurie Jr., Guest
  WABD—Starlit Time, Variety
  WJZ-TV—Think Fast—Quiz
  WPIX—News—John Tillman
  WATV—Western Film
:15-WPIX—Voice of the People
:30-WCBS-TV—This Is Show Business,
    With Clifton Fadiman, Abe
    Burrows, George S. Kaufman,
    Larraine Day, Jack Leonard, Bidu
    Sayao, Johnny Johnson
  WNBT—The Aldrich Family—
    Comedy, With Dick Tyler, Jackie
    Kelk, Nancy Carroll, Others
  WJZ-TV—Diane Doxee Show
:00-WCBS-TV—Toast of the Town: Ed
    Sullivan, Hedy Lamarr, Pat
    O'Brien, Mimi Benzell, Others
  WNBT—Comedy Hour: With Dean
    Martin and Jerry Lewis: Valerie
    Bettis, Marilyn Maxwell, Others
  WABD—Rhythm Rodeo, With Art
    Jarrett
  WJZ-TV—The Ruggles, Comedy
  WATV—Feature Film
  WPIX—Double Feature Theatre
:30-WABD—Film Feature
  WJZ-TV—Sit or Miss Game
  WCBS-TV—Robert Q. Lewis Show
  WNBT—Television Playhouse: The

Long Run, With Francis Lederer,
    Vickie Cummings
  WABD—They Stand Accused
  WJZ-TV—Stage Two Revue
  WATV—Western Film
9:15-WCBS-TV—Three's Company
9:30-WCBS-TV—Documentary: The Facts
    We Face
  WJZ-TV—Faith for Today
10:00-WCBS-TV—John Daly, News; Brig.
    Gen. Frank Howley, Guest
  WNBT—Garroway at Large
  WABD—Yesterday's Newsreel
  WJZ-TV—Film: The Marshall Plan
  WPIX—Telenews Weekly
  WATV—Feature Film
10:15-WCBS-TV—Film Theatre: Monster
    Maker, With J. Carroll Naish,
    Ralph Morgan, Wanda McKay
10:30-WNBT—To Be Announced
  WPIX—Mayfair House Movies: A
    Star Is Born, With Janet Gaynor,
    Frederic March
11:00-WNBT—News Review of the Week
  WATV—Feature Film
12:15-WPIX—Telepix News

MONDAY, SEPTEMBER 18

9:30-WNBT—Johnny Andrews Show
  WABD—News, Ed Condit
9:45-WNBT—Josephine McCarthy, Cooking
  WABD—Morning Chapel
10:00-WNBT—Kathi Norris Show
  WABD—Baby Sitter-Pat Meikle
10:30-WABD—Kitchen Fare—Susan Adams
11:00-WNBT—Date in Manhattan
  WABD—Television Shopper
11:30-WJZ-TV—The Fitzgeralds
11:45-WNBT—News Bob Wilson
12:00-WNBT—Carl Caruso
  WABD—Headline Clues
  WJZ-TV—Kitchen Kapers
  WPIX—Music: Newsreel
12:30-WABD—Johnny Olsen Rumpus Room
  WJZ-TV—Market Melodies
  WPIX—Batter Up—Hal Tunis
12:45-WOR—Comedy Carnival
1:00-WNBT—News Summary
  WABD—Okay Mother—Dennis James
  WOR-TV—Felton's Knothole Gang
  WPIX—Laraine Day Show
1:15-WCBS-TV—Facts and Forecasts
1:20-WPIX—Baseball: St. Louis vs.
    Giants, at Polo Grounds
1:25-WOR-TV—Baseball: Dodgers vs.
    Chicago, at Ebbets Field
1:30-WCBS-TV—About the House—Lydia
    Rogers, Woody Klose
  WABD—Sidewalk Interviews
  WATV—Home Economics—Ruth Bean
1:45-WABD—Susan Raye, Songs
2:00-WATV—Feature Film
2:30-WCBS-TV—The Real McKay
  WJZ-TV—Telephone Game
3:00-WJZ-TV—Zeke Manners Show
  WATV—Homemaker's Guide
3:30-WCBS-TV—Look Your Best, With
    Richard Willis
  WNBT—Racing From Belmont Park
4:00-WCBS-TV—Homemakers' Exchange
  WATV—Western Film
4:30-WCBS-TV—Vanity Fair
  WOR-TV—Clubhouse Quiz
  WPIX—Ted Steele Show
5:00-WCBS-TV—Lucky Pup
  WNBT—NBC Comics
  WJZ-TV—Mr. Magic
  WATV—Junior Frolics
5:15-WCBS-TV—Life With Snarky Parker
  WNBT—Panhandle Pete and Jenni-
    fer—Children's Show
  WJZ-TV—Paddy Pelican
5:30-WCBS-TV—The Chuck Wagon
  WNBT—Howdy Doody
  WABD—Serial Theatre
  WJZ-TV—Hold 'Er Newt
  WPIX—Six Gun Playhouse
  WATV—Feature Film
5:45-WJZ-TV—Space Patrol—Sketch
6:00-WNBT—Easy Does It—Variety
  WABD—Small Fry Club
6:25-WNBT-News Don Goddard

6:30-WNBT—Tex and Jinx Interviews
  WABD—Magic Cottage-Pat Meikle
  WPIX—News; Weather
  WATV—Texas Jim Robertson, Songs
6:45-WCBS-TV—Bob Howard Show
  WPIX—Jimmy Powers
  WATV—Western Short
6:55-WNBT—Weather Man
7:00-WCBS-TV—Garry Moore Show
  WNBT—Kukla, Fran and Ollie
  WJZ-TV—News: Club Seven
  WOR-TV—Camera on Korea
  WPIX—News, John Tillman
  WATV—Western Film
7:15-WPIX—Film: Broadway Limited,
    With Dennis O'Keefe
7:30-WCBS-TV—Television News
  WNBT—Roberta Quinlan Show
  WABD—Manhattan Spotlight
  WJZ-TV—Hollywood Screen Test
  WOR-TV—Comedy Carnival
7:45-WCBS-TV—The Stork Club
  WNBT—News Caravan
  WABD—Hazel Scott, Songs
  WOR-TV—Film: Riders of Destiny,
    With John Wayne
8:00-WCBS-TV—Pantomime Quiz
  WNBT—Paul Winchell-Jerry Ma-
    honey Show
  WABD—Armed Forces Film
  WJZ-TV—Treasury Men in Action
  WATV—Feature Film
8:30-WCBS-TV—Godfrey's Talent Scouts
  WNBT—Lily Pons, Soprano
  WABD—Al Morgan Show
  WJZ-TV—Author Meets the Critics
  WPIX—To Be Announced
  WATV—Finals of Miss Television,
    1950, Contest
8:45-WOR-TV—Film: Accused, With Do-
    lores Del Rio, Douglas Fairbanks Jr.
9:00-WCBS-TV—Candid Camera
  WNBT—Lights Out: Leopard Lady,
    With Boris Karloff
  WABD—Wrestling, Columbia Park
  WJZ-TV—Double Feature Film
9:30-WCBS-TV—We Take Your Word
  WNBT—To Be Announced
10:00-WCBS-TV—Studio One: Trilby, With
    Priscilla Gillette, Arnold Moss
10:15-WOR-TV—Top View in Sports
10:30-WNBT—Talent Search—Skitch
    Henderson
11:00-WCBS-TV—At Home Show: Earl
    Wrightson, Baritone
  WNBT—Broadway Open House
  WPIX—News; Weather; Sports
  WATV—Star Dust Theatre
11:15-WCBS-TV—Allan Jackson, News
11:25-WCBS-TV—Midnight Snack, Variety
11:30-WPIX—Gail and Bill, Songs
11:45-WPIX—Night Owl Theatre
12:00-WATV—Western Short

TUESDAY, SEPTEMBER 19

9:30-WNBT—Johnny Andrews, Piano
  WABD—News—Ed Condit
9:45-WNBT—Josephine McCarthy Show
  WABD—Morning Chapel
10:00-WNBT—Kathi Norris Show
  WABD—Baby Sitter
10:30-WABD—Kitchen Fare—Susan Adams
11:00-WNBT—Date in Manhattan
  WABD—Television Shopper
11:30-WJZ-TV—The Fitzgeralds
11:45-WNBT—News-Bob Wilson
12:00-WNBT—Carl Caruso Program
  WABD—Headline Clues
  WJZ-TV—Kitchen Kapers
12:30-WABD—Johnny Olsen Rumpus Room
  WJZ-TV—Market Melodies
  WPIX—Batter Up-Hal Tunis
1:00-WNBT—News Summary
  WABD—Okay, Mother—Dennis James
  WOR-TV—Felton's Knothole Gang
  WPIX—Laraine Day Program
1:15-WCBS-TV—Facts and Forecasts
1:20-WPIX—Baseball: Cincinnati vs.
    Giants, at Polo Grounds
1:25-WOR-TV—Baseball: Dodgers vs
    Pittsburgh at Ebbets Field

1:30-WCBS-TV—About the House. With
    Lydia Rogers, Woody Klose
    WABD—Sidewalk interviews
    WATV—Home Economics, Ruth Bean
1:45-WABD—Susan Raye, Songs
2:00-WATV—Feature Film
2:30-WCBS-TV—The Real McKay
    WJZ-TV—Telephone Game
3:00-WCBS-TV, WNBT, N. General
    Assembly, Flushing
    WJZ-TV—Zeke Manners Show
    WATV—Homemakers Guide
4:00-WCBS-TV—Homemakers' Exchange
    WATV—Western Film
4:30-WCBS-TV—Vanity Fair
    WPIX—Ted Steele Show
5:00-WCBS-TV—Lucky Pup
    WNBT—NBC Comics
    WJZ-TV—Mr. Magic
    WATV—Junior Frolics
5:15-WCBS-TV—Life with Snarky Parker
    WNBT—Panhandle Pete and Jennifer
    —Children's Show
    WJZ-TV—Paddy Pelican
5:30-WCBS-TV—The Chuck Wagon
    WNBT—Howdy Doody
    WABD—Serial Theatre
    WJZ-TV—Hold 'er Newt
    WPIX—Six-Gun Playhouse
    WATV—Feature Film
5:45-WJZ-TV—Space Patrol—Sketch
6:00-WNBT—Easy Does It—Variety
    WABD—Small Fry Club
6:25-WNBT—News; Don Goddard
6:30-WNBT—Tex and Jinx Interviews
    WABD—Magic Cottage—Pat Meikle
    WOR-TV—Mystery Rider
    WPIX—News; Weather
    WATV—Texas Jim Robertson, Songs
6:45-WCBS-TV—Bob Howard Show
    WOR-TV—Time for Beany
    WPIX—Jimmy Powers
    WATV—Western Films
6:55-WNBT—Weather Man
7:00-WCBS-TV—Garry Moore Show
    WNBT—Kukla, Fran and Ollie
    WABD—Captain Video
    WJZ-TV—News; Club Seven
    WOR-TV—Comedy Carnival
    WPIX—News—John Tillman
7:15-WOR-TV—Mr. and Mrs. Mystery
    WPIX—Film: Scattergood Survives
    a Murder, With Guy Kibbee
7:30-WCBS-TV—Television News
    WNBT—John Conte Little Show
    WABD—Eloise Salutes the Stars
    WJZ-TV—Buster Keaton—Film
    WOR-TV—Western Playhouse
7:45-WCBS-TV—Three's Company
    WNBT—News Caravan
    WABD—Joan Edwards Show
8:00-WCBS-TV—Sure as Fate: Run
    From The Sun, With Robert Cum-
    mings: Jean Gillespie
    WNBT—Star Theatre, With Milton
    Berle, Charles Coburn, Robert
    Alda, Others
    WABD—Court of Current Issues
    WJZ-TV—Buck Rogers—Sketch
    WOR-TV—Bowery Music Hall. With
    Jack Linder
    WATV—To Be Announced
8:30-WJZ-TV—Mysteries of Chinatown
    WPIX—News; Sports
9:00-WCBS-TV—Winner Take All
    WNBT—Fireside Theatre: Incident
    in the Rain, With Irene Vernon,
    Warren Douglass, Frances Williams
    WABD—Cavalcade of Bands
    WJZ-TV—Your Witness
    WOR-TV—Wrestling From Bronx
    Winter Garden
    WPIX—To Be Announced
    WATV—Stock Car Races
9:30-WCBS-TV—Suspense
    WNBT—Circle Theatre: The Other
    Woman, With Louise Albritton,
    Glenn Langan
    WJZ-TV—Motorboat Racing Film
10:00-WCBS-TV—Play: The Black Door,
    With Dane Clark
    WNBT—Amateur Hour—Ted Mack
    WABD—Star Time With Frances
    Langford, Benny Goodman, Lew
    Parker; Others
    WJZ-TV—Roller Derby
10:30-WCBS-TV—Red Barber's Clubhouse
10:45-WCBS-TV—Ned Calmer, Interviews
11:00-WCBS-TV—Alan Jackson, News

WNBT—Broadway Open House
WABD—Film: When Knights Were
    Bold, With Jack Buchanan, Fay
    Wray
WOR-TV—Starlit Playhouse
WPIX—News; Weather; Sports
WATV—Stardust Theatre
11:10-WCBS-TV—Midnight Snack, Variety
11:30-WPIX—Gail and Bill, Songs
11:45-WPIX—Night Owl Theatre
12:00-WATV—Western Short

WEDNESDAY, SEPTEMBER 20

9:30-WNBT—Johnny Andrews, Piano
    WABD—News—Ed Condit
9:45-WNBT—Josephine McCarthy,
    Cooking Show
    WABD—Morning Chapel
10:00-WNBT—Kathi Norris Show
    WABD—Baby Sitter
10:30-WABD—Kitchen Fare—Susan Adam
11:00-WNBT—Date in Manhattan
    WABD—Television Shopper
11:30-WJZ-TV—The Fitzgeralds
11:45-WNBT—News—Bob Wilson
12:00-WNBT—Carl Caruso Program
    WABD—Headline Clues
    WJZ-TV—Kitchen Kapers
12:30-WABD—Johnny Olson Rumpus Room
    WJZ-TV—Market Melodies
    WPIX—Batter Up—Hal Tunis
1:00-WNBT—News Summary
    WABD—Okay Mother—Dennis James
    WOR-TV—Felton's Knothole Gang
    WPIX—Laraine Day Show
1:15-WCBS-TV—Facts and Forecasts
1:20-WPIX—Baseball: Cincinnati vs.
    Giants, at Polo Grounds
1:25-WOR-TV—Baseball: Dodgers vs.
    Pittsburgh, at Ebbets Field
1:30-WCBS-TV—About the House, With
    Lydia Rogers, Woody Klose
    WABD—Sidewalk Interviews
    WATV—Home Economics, Ruth Bean
1:45-WABD—Susan Raye, Songs
2:00-WATV—Feature Film
2:30-WCBS-TV—The Real McKay
    WJZ-TV—Telephone Game
3:00-WJZ-TV—Zeke Manners Show
    WATV—Homemakers Guide
3:30-WCBS-TV—Look Your Best, with
    Richard Willis
4:00-WCBS-TV—Homemakers Exchange
    WNBT—Racing from Aqueduct
    WATV—Western Film
4:30-WCBS-TV—Vanity Fair
    WOR-TV—Clubhouse Quiz—Bob Edge
    WPIX—Ted Steele Show
5:00-WCBS-TV—Lucky Pup
    WNBT—NBC Comics
    WJZ-TV—Mr. Magic
    WOR-TV—Starlit Matinee
    WATV—Junior Frolics
5:15-WCBS-TV—Life With Snarky Parker
    WNBT—Panhandle Pete and Jenni-
    fer—Children's Show
    WJZ-TV—Paddy Pelican
5:30-WCBS-TV—The Chuck Wagon
    WNBT—Howdy Doody
    WABD—Serial Theatre
    WJZ-TV—Hold 'Er Newt
    WPIX—Six Gun Playhouse
    WATV—Feature Films
5:45-WJZ-TV—Space Patrol—Sketch
6:00-WNBT—Easy Does It, Variety
    WABD—Small Fry Club
6:25-WNBT—News—Don Goddard
6:30-WNBT—Tex and Jinx Interviews
    WABD—Magic Cottage—Pat Meikle
    WOR-TV—Mystery Rider
    WPIX—News; Weather
    WATV—Texas Jim Robertson, Songs
6:45-WCBS-TV—Bob Howard Show
    WOR-TV—Time for Beany
    WPIX—Jimmy Powers
    WATV—Western Short
6:55-WNBT—Weather—Tex Antoine
7:00-WCBS-TV—Jeanne Bargy Show
    WNBT—Kukla, Fran and Ollie
    WABD—Captain Video—Sketch
    WJZ-TV—News; Club Seven
    WOR-TV—Comedy Carnival
    WPIX—News—John Tillman
    WATV—Western Film
7:15-WOR-TV—Mr. and Mrs. Mystery
    WPIX—Film: Pack Up Your Troubles
7:30-WCBS-TV—Television News
    WNBT—Roberta Quinlan

WABD—Manhattan Spotlight
WJZ-TV—Chance of a Lifetime
    With John Reed King
WOR-TV—Dinner at Sardi's
7:45-WCBS-TV—The Stork Club
    WNBT—News Caravan
    WABD—Hazel Scott, Songs
8:00-WCBS-TV—Gary Moore Show
    WNBT—The Nature of Things
    WABD—Film: Criminals Within
    with Eric Linden, Ann Doran
    WOR-TV—What's Offered?
    WJZ-TV—On Trial
    WATV—Feature Film
8:15-WNBT—Wendy Barrie Show
8:30-WNBT—Cameo Theatre: The P
    Sack, with Dennis Harrison, G
    Gordon, James Little
    WJZ-TV—Film: Dick Tracy
    WOR-TV—Tiny Fairbanks Show
8:45-WOR-TV—Today's News and Sp
9:00-WCBS-TV—Twine Time
    WNBT—Television Theatre:
    Stop, with Mildred Dunnock,
    bel Price
    WABD—Famous Jury Trials
    WJZ-TV—Don McNeil TV Club
    WOR-TV—Wrestling, Coney Islan
    Velodrome
    WATV—Western Film
9:30-WCBS-TV—The Web: Murder's
    Challenge
    WABD—The Plainclothes Man—N
    WPIX—Art Ford Show
10:00-WCBS-TV—Film: Shake Hands V
    Murder, with Iris Adrian, Fr
    Jenks, Douglas Fowley
    WNBT—Break the Bank
    WABD—Broadway to Hollywood
    WJZ-TV—Wrestling, from Chica
    WATV—Broadway Theatre
10:30-WNBT—Stars Over Hollywood:
    Girl or Ghost, with Gloria
    Saunders
    WABD—Yesterday's Newsreel
11:00-WCBS-TV—News—Allen Jackson
    WNBT—Broadway Open House
    WCR-TV—Starlit Playhouse
    WPIX—News; Weather; Sports
    WATV—Stardust Theatre
11:10-WCBS-TV—Midnight Snack, Vari
11:30-WPIX—Gail and Bill, Songs
11:45-WPIX—Night Owl Theatre
12:00-WATV—Western Short

THURSDAY, SEPTEMBER 21

9:30-WNBT—Johnny Andrews, Piano
    WABD—News—Ed Condit
9:45-WNBT—Josephine McCarthy
    Cooking Show
    WABD—Morning Chapel
10:00-WNBT—Kathi Norris Show
    WABD—Baby Sitter
10:30-WNBT—Kitchen Fare—Susan Ada
11:00-WNBT—Date in Manhattan
    WABD—Television Shopper
11:30-WJZ-TV—The Fitzgeralds
11:45-WNBT—News—Bob Wilson
12:00-WNBT—Carl Caruso Program
    WABD—Headline Clues
    WJZ-TV—Kitchen Kapers
12:30-WABD—Johnny Olsen Rumpus Ro
    WJZ-TV—Market Melodies
    WPIX—Batter Up—Hal Tunis
1:00-WNBT—News Summary
    WABD—Okay Mother—Dennis Jan
    WPIX—Laraine Day Show
    WOR-TV—Felton's Knothole Gan
1:15-WCBS-TV—Facts and Forecasts
1:20-WPIX—Baseball: Cincinnati vs.
    Giants, at Polo Grounds
1:25-WOR-TV—Baseball: Dodgers vs.
    Pittsburgh, at Ebbets Field
1:30-WCBS-TV—About the House, Wi
    Lydia Rogers, Woody Kluse
    WABD—Susan Adams Kitchen
    WATV—Home Economics—Ruth Be
1:45-WABD—Susan Raye, Songs
2:00-WATV—Feature Film
2:30-WCBS-TV—The Real McKay
    WJZ-TV—Telephone Game
3:00-WJZ-TV—Zeke Manners Show
    WATV—Homemaker's Guide
4:00-WCBS-TV—Homemakers' Exchange
    WATV—Western Film
4:30-WCBS-TV—Vanity Fair
    WPIX—Ted Steele Show
    WOR-TV—Clubhouse Quiz, Bob Ed

52

WCBS-TV—Lucky Pup
WNBT—NBC Comics
WJZ-TV—Mr. Magic
WATV—Junior Frolics
WCBS-TV—Life With Snarky Parker
WNBT—Panhandle Pete and Jennifer—Children's Show
WJZ-TV—Paddy Pelican
WCBS-TV—The Chuck Wagon
WNBT—Howdy Doody
WABD—Serial Theatre
WJZ-TV—Hold 'er Newt
WPIX—Six-Gun Playhouse
WATV—Feature Film
WJZ-TV—Space Patrol—Sketch
WNBT—Friendship Ranch—Variety
WNBT—Easy Does It—Variety
WNBT—News: Don Goddard
WNBT—Tex and Jinx—Interviews
WABD—Magic Cottage—Pat Meikle
WOR-TV—Mystery Rider
WPIX—News; Weather
WATV—Texas Jim Robertson, Songs
WCBS-TV—Bob Howard Show
WOR-TV—Time for Beany
WPIX—Jimmy Powers
WATV—Western Films
WNET—The Weatherman
WCBS-TV—Garry Moore Show
WNBT—Kukla, Fran and Ollie
WABD—Captain Video
WJZ-TV—News; Club Seven
WOR-TV—Comedy Carnival
WPIX—News; Gail and Bill, Songs
WOR-TV—Mr. and Mrs. Mystery
WJZ-TV—Kiernan's Kaleidoscope
WCBS-TV—Television News
WNBT—John Conte's Little Show
WABD—Manhattan Spotlight
WJZ-TV—The Lone Ranger
WOR-TV—Let's Arbitrate
WPIX—Play—Leave It to Papa
WCBS-TV—Three's Company
WNBT—News Caravan
WABD—Joan Edwards, Songs
WCBS-TV—The Show Goes On
WNBT—Believe It or Not
WABD—Film: Mystery of the Thirteenth Guest, With Dick Purcell, Helen Parrish
WJZ-TV—Stop the Music
WOR-TV—Al Siegal's Music Shop
WPIX—Dixie Showboat
WATV—Stairway to Stardom
WNBT—Hawkins Falls
WOR-TV—News and Sports
WPIX—To Be Announced
WOR-TV—Boxing, Fort Hamilton
WCBS-TV—Alan Young Show; Jane Froman, Guest
WNBT—Jack Haley Show
WABD—Morey Amsterdam Show
WJZ-TV—Holiday Hotel—Comedy, With Don Ameche
WPIX—Wrestling—Ridgewood Grove
WATV—Western Film
WCBS-TV—Starlight Theatre
WABD—To Be Announced
WJZ-TV—Blind Date
WCBS-TV—Truth or Consequences
WNBT—Martin Kane, Private Eye—Play, With Bill Gargan
WJZ-TV—Roller Derby
WATV—Feature Film
WCBS-TV—Play: The Double Dyed Deceiver With Ian Keith, Ralph Rigg
WNBT—Quick on the Draw
WCBS-TV—Allen Jackson, News
WNBT—Broadway Open House
WOR-TV—Starlit Playhouse
WPIX—News; weather
WATV—Stardust Theatre
WCBS-TV—Midnight Snack, Variety
WJZ-TV—Red Grange Predicts
WPIX—Night Owl Theatre
WATV—Western Short

FRIDAY, SEPTEMBER 22

WNBT—Johnny Andrews, Piano
WABD—News—Ed Condit
WABD—Josephine McCarthy
WABD—Morning Chapel
WNBT—Kathi Norris Show
WABD—Baby Sitter
WABD—Betsy Brewster's Kitchen
WNBT—Date in Manhattan
WABD—Television Shopper

11:30-WJZ-TV—The Fitzgeralds
11:45-WNBT—News—Bob Wilson
12:00-WNBT—Anne Pringle—Carl Caruso
WABD—Headline Clues
WJZ-TV—Kitchen Kapers
WPIX—Music; Newsreel
12:30-WABD—Johnny Olsen Rumpus Room
WJZ-TV—Market Melodies
12:45-WPIX—Matinee Movie
1:00-WNBT—News Summary
WABD—Okay Mother—Dennis James
WJZ-TV—Cooking—Dione Lucas
1:15-WCBS-TV—Facts and Forecasts
1:30-WCBS-TV—About the House, With Lydia Rogers, Woody Klose
WABD—Sidewalk Interviews
WJZ-TV—Market Melodies
WATV—Home Economics—Ruth Bean
1:45-WABD—Susan Raye, Songs
2:00-WATV—Feature Film
WPIX—Ted Steele Show
2:30-WCBS-TV—The Real McKay
WJZ-TV—Telephone Game
3:00-WCBS-TV—Zeke Manners Show
WATV—Homemakers' Guide
3:30-WCBS-TV—Look Your Best, with Richard Willis
4:00-WCBS-TV—Homemakers' Exchange
WATV—Feature Film
4:30-WCBS-TV—Vanity Fair
5:00-WCBS-TV—Lucky Pup
WNBT—NBC Comics
WJZ-TV—Mr. Magic
WPIX—News; Glenn's Bandwagon
WATV—Junior Frolics
5:15-WCBS-TV—Life With Snarky Parker,
WNBT—Panhandle Pete and Jennifer—Children's Show
WJZ-TV—Paddy Pelican
5:30-WCBS-TV—The Chuck Wagon
WNBT—Howdy Doody
WABD—Serial Theatre
WJZ-TV—Hold 'er Newt
WPIX—Six Gun Playhouse
WATV—Feature Film
5:45-WJZ-TV—Space Patrol—Sketch
6:00-WNTB—Easy Does It—Variety
WABD—Small Fry Club
6:25-WNBT—News—Don Goddard
6:30-WNBT—Tex and Jinx—Interviews
WABD—Magic Cottage—Pat Meikle
WOR-TV—The Mystery Rider
WPIX—News; Weather
WATV—Texas Jim Robertson, Songs
6:45-WCBS-TV—Bob Howard Show
WOR-TV—Time for Beany
WPIX—Jimmy Powers
WATV—Weather Films
6:55-WNBT—Weatherman—Tex Antoine
7:00-WCBS-TV—Garry Moore Show
WNBT—Kukla, Fran and Ollie
WABD—Captain Video
WJZ-TV—News; Club Seven
WOR-TV—Comedy Carnival
WPIX—News—John Tillman
7:15-WOR-TV—Mr. and Mrs. Mystery
WPIX—Film: It Happened in New Orleans, With Benita Hume
7:30-WCBS-TV—Television News
WNBT—Roberta Quinlan Show
WABD—Manhattan Spotlight
WJZ-TV—Corrigan's Ranch, Variety
WOR-TV—Bobby Benson—Sketch
7:45-WCBS-TV—The Stork Club
WNBT—News Caravan
WABD—Hazel Scott, Songs
8:00-WNBT—Mama, With Peggy Wood
WNBT—The Quiz Kids
WABD—To Be Announced
WJZ-TV—My True Story
WOR-TV—Twenty Questions
WATV—News; Film Short
8:30-WCBS-TV—Detective's Wife—Play, With Lynn Bari, Donald Curtis
WNBT—We, the People
WABD—Hold That Camera
WJZ-TV—Football Giants Huddle
WOR-TV—Play: Trapped
WPIX—Football: Boston College vs. Wake Forest, at Braves Field, Boston
8:35-WATV—Wrestling Matches, From Meadowbrook Bowl
9:00-WCBS-TV—Theatre Hour: The Married Look, With Paul Kelly
WNBT—Versatile Varieties
WABD—Hands of Mystery
WOR-TV—Library of Art Films

WOR-TV—Wrestling, Jamaica Arena
9:30-WNBT—The Clock: The Morning After, With Raymond Massey, Mady Christians
WABD—Roscoe Karns, Inside Detective—Sketch
WJZ-TV—Tin Pan Alley TV
10:00-WCBS-TV—Star of the Family, With Morton Downey
WNBT—Boxing: Madison Square Garden
WABD—Cavalcade of Stars
WJZ-TV—Penthouse Party
10:30-WCBS-TV—By Popular Demand, With Arlene Francis
WJZ-TV—Mystery Film
10:45-WNBT—Fights of the Century
11:00-WCBS-TV—Alan Dale Show
WNBT—Broadway Open House
WABD—John Feeney Show
WOR-TV—Starlit Playhouse
WPIX—News; Weather; Sports
WATV—Stardust Theatre
11:30-WCBS-TV—Allan Jackson, News
WPIX—Gail and Bill, Songs
11:40-WCBS-TV—Midnight Snack, Variety
11:45-WPIX—Night Owl Theatre
12:00-WATV—Western Short

SATURDAY, SEPTEMBER 23

11:00 A.M.-WJZ-TV—Saturday at the Zoo
11:30-WJZ-TV—Acrobat Ranch
12:00-WJZ-TV—Animal Clinic
WPIX—Music; Newsreel
12:45-WPIX—Matinee Movie
1:00-WATV—Of Human Interest
1:45-WABD—Dizzy Dean
1:55-WABD—Baseball: Yankees vs. Boston, at Yankee Stadium
2:00-WPIX—Ted Steele Show
2:30-WPIX—Football: Yale vs. Connecticut, at New Haven
3:00-WATV—Feature Film
3:30-WNBT—Horse Racing, Aqueduct
4:00-WATV—Western Film
4:30-WABD—Dizzy Dean
5:00-WOR-TV—Italian Feature Film
WPIX—News; Glenn's Bandwagon
WATV—Junior Frolics
5:30-WNET—Joe DiMaggio Show
WPIX—Six Gun Playhouse
5:45-WNBT—To Be Announced
6:00-WABD—Frontier Theatre: Lion's Den, With Tim McCoy
WATV—Feature Film
6:15-WCBS-TV—Week in Review
6:30-WCBS-TV—Lucky Pup
WNBT—Smilin' Ed McConnell and His Gang
WOR-TV—Mystery Rider
WPIX—Sports Telecade; Films
6:45-WOR-TV—Time for Beany
WPIX—Jimmy Powers
7:00-WCBS-TV—The Big Top
WNBT—Hank McCune Show
WABD—Captain Video
WOR-TV—Comedy Carnival
WPIX—News; John Tillman
WATV—Western Film
7:15-WOR-TV—Mr. and Mrs. Mystery
WPIX—Film: Oliver Twist
7:30-WNBT—One Man's Family—Drama
WABD—Film: Woman in the Hall, With Ursula Jean, Jean Simmons
WJZ-TV—Film: Marshall of Gunsight Pass
WOR-TV—Talent Parade
8:00-WCBS-TV—Beat the Clock
WNBT—Saturday Night Revue: Jack Carter Show
WJZ-TV—Paul Whiteman, Teen Club
WATV—Your Congressman
8:30-WOR-TV—Today's News and Sports
WPIX—To Be Announced
WATV—Stock Car Races
8:45-WOR-TV—Johnny Farrell Golf Club
9:00-WCBS-TV—Premiere Playhouse
WNBT—Sid Caesar—Imogene Coca
WABD—Country Style, Variety
WJZ-TV—Roller Derby
WPIX—Boxing, Ridgewood Grove
10:00-WABD—Wrestling From Chicago
10:30-WNBT—To Be Announced
11:00-WOR-TV—Starlit Playhouse
WPIX—News; Weather, Music
WATV—Stardust Theatre
11:30-WPIX—Night Owl Theatre

WNBT CHANNEL 4

THE NEW YORK TIMES, SUNDAY, SEPTEMBER 17, 1950.

a strapping singer and a startling gad-fly

DEAN MARTIN & JERRY LEWIS

starring in a great revue

COLGATE COMEDY HOUR

and great viewing all night long

4:30	Meet The Press		**8:00**	Colgate Comedy Hour
5:00	Watch The World		**9:00**	Philco Television Playhouse presents THE LONG RUN starring Francis Lederer
5:30	Hopalong Cassidy			
6:30	Say It With Acting			
7:00	Leave It To The Girls		**10:00**	Garroway At Large
7:30	Aldrich Family		**10:30**	This Week's News in Review

(The year's headlines . . .)

1950

NORTH KOREAN COMMUNISTS IN-
VADE SOUTH . . . . TRUMAN ORDERS
MACARTHUR TO KOREA . . . . UNITED
NATIONS FORMS ARMY TO REPEL COM-
MUNIST INVASION OF SOUTH KOREA
. . . . FORMOSA NEUTRALIZED BY U.S.
7TH FLEET . . . . CHINESE COMMUNISTS
INVADE SOUTH KOREA . . . . MAC-
ARTHUR CROSSES 38TH PARALLEL IN-
TO NORTH KOREA . . . . CHINESE DRIVE
UN FORCES BELOW 38TH . . . .

. . . Meanwhile, on TV . . .

WHAT'S MY LINE?

The granddaddy of all TV quiz panel shows, *What's My Line?*, made its television debut on February 2, 1950, with columnist Dorothy Kilgallen, actress Arlene Francis and humorist Hal Block and Louis Untermeyer constituting the panel that tried to guess the occupations of contestants. John Daly was the show's moderator and host. Sunday night on CBS was *What's My Lines'?* permanent address for almost twenty years. When Block and Untermeyer left the show, they were replaced by Bennett Cerf and Fred Allen, whose slot was filled by Steve Allen after his death. Cerf and the Misses Kilgallen and Francis were permanent panelists the majority of years the show was on network TV. The producing team of Goodson and Todman, who also produced most of television's other panel shows, syndicated their *What's My Line?* program after CBS canceled the long-running show.

What's My Line? panelists Bennett Cerf, Arlene Francis, Dorothy Kilgallen and Fred Allen with moderator John Daly.

JACK BENNY

By 1950 the handwriting was on the wall as far as radio broadcasting was concerned, and many of that medium's stars were somewhat reluctantly making their moves to TV. Jack Benny, one of radio's brightest stars, made his TV debut in October, 1950, bringing with him most of his popular radio cast. Rochester (Eddie Anderson), announcer Don Wilson, vocalist Dennis Day and Jack's wife, Mary Livingston (who was less enthusiastic about TV than radio) all turned up. Benny's TV show was more variety than situation comedy, and Jack concentrated on introducing show-business celebrities from the movies and radio to TV audiences. Actress Marilyn Monroe and singer Johnny Ray were just two of the stars who made their TV debuts on *The Jack Benny Show*. In 1960 Jack decided to drop the weekly TV grind and has since concentrated on specials and occasional guest appearances.

On Jack Benny's first TV show, he appeared as a violin-playing hillbilly, to the delight of his watching audience.

YOU BET YOUR LIFE

You Bet Your Life **star Groucho and his famed duck.**

Groucho Marx deserted famed brothers Harpo and Chico when, in 1950, he became the star of his own weekly television series, *You Bet Your Life*. The show, a comedy-quiz program, had remarkable staying power on TV considering its simple format. With his announcer, George Fenneman, who was often the butt of Groucho's caustic remarks, cigar-puffing, bushy-mustached Groucho asked contestants impossible questions. Should they say the "secret word," a strange-looking duck would appear with a beakful of money. The show remained on the air well into the sixties.

Announcer George Fenneman and Groucho.

GARRY MOORE SHOW

A popular daytime variety show was MC'd by former Jimmy Durante sidekick Garry Moore and presented by CBS in 1950. Denise Lor, Ken Carson and Durward Kirby were regulars on the show, which remained on the air until 1958. That year, Moore became the star of a nighttime series—a weekly hour-long variety-music show which featured comediennes Marion Lorne and Carol Burnett, as well as old standby Durward Kirby. When the sensational Miss Burnett left the show in the mid-1960's, it lost much of its luster, and Garry retired from television for several years to rest and recuperate from the grueling weekly TV grind. He has since returned to television as MC of a syndicated quiz show and can also be seen as a guest star on

Moore's 1958 nighttime variety show comes to a close. Seen left to right, regulars Marion Lorne and Durward Kirby, guest Mahalia Jackson, Garry, guests Marge and Gower Champion and regular Carol Burnett.

such shows as Miss Burnett's own weekly comedy series.

Garry Moore's 1950 daytime show featured musical director Howard Smith, announcer Durward Kirby, Garry, singers Denise Lor and Ken Carson.

THE KATE SMITH HOUR

Early-afternoon television was graced in 1950 by the presence of Miss Kate Smith. NBC brought the former leading light of radio before TV cameras in a combination chatter, interview and song show, directed to the ladies of the house. Kate's longtime manager and friend, Ted Collins, was on hand with Kate, and an impressive list of guest stars from the world of show business appeared on the program. Miss Smith's TV popularity was such that NBC rewarded her with an evening musical-variety show, which ran in conjunction with the daytime show. Since 1954, when Kate's shows left the air, she has been seen regularly as a guest star on most of television's leading comedy-variety programs.

Ted Collins and Kate Smith are seen with Jeff Clark, one of the many guests on *The Kate Smith Hour.*

BURNS AND ALLEN

Radio stars George Burns and Gracie Allen, a celebrated husband and wife comedy team who had begun their careers as vaudeville performers in the 1920's, brought their famous routines to television in 1950, in a weekly situation comedy series on CBS. Cast regulars, Bea Benadaret as next door neighbor Blanche Norton, Larry Keaton as Blanche's husband, Harry, announcer Harry Von Zell and the Burnses' son, Ronny, were on hand to add to the comedy of the program. Gracie left the show because of ill health in 1958, and one year later the show retired from the air. Few viewers will forget the gruff, lovable George and his cigar-smoking monologues, which were mostly about Gracie, the muddleheaded queen with a strange kind of logic all her own.

George Burns and Gracie Allen

COLGATE COMEDY HOUR

The Colgate Comedy Hour, first seen in 1950, presented some of the biggest names in show business as hosts on an alternating basis. Some of the notables to serve in this capacity were Dean Martin and Jerry Lewis, Fred Allen, Eddie Cantor, Jimmy Durante, Abbott and Costello, Spike Jones and his City Slickers and Bob Hope. The list of guest stars who also appeared on this series included Martha Raye, Tennessee Ernie Ford, Jack Carter and Perry Como. Every now and then a special full-length musical comedy was presented. Musical comedy star Ethel Merman appeared in a special telecast of *Anything Goes,* and Bobby Clark was seen in *The Would-be Gentleman.* Other special attractions of the *Comedy Hour* included a presentation of *Ice Capades of 1954* with Donna Atwood.

Elaine May and Mike Nichols were featured on the *Comedy Hour* before both went their separate ways to become leading writers and directors.

Jerry Lewis and Dean Martin were *Colgate Comedy Hour* hosts.

THE ROY ROGERS SHOW

Cowboy star Roy Rogers, accompanied by his wife, Dale Evans, his horse, Trigger, and his dog, Bullet, also arrived on the television scene in 1950. His show, a combination songfest and adventure series proved popular with the small fry and enjoyed a long, successful TV stay.

Roy Rogers, his horse, Trigger, and his wife, Dale Evans, in the syndicated *Roy Rogers Show.*

ROOTIE KAZOOTIE

Hand puppet Rootie Kazootie, his baseball cap tipped to one side, and his pal, Todd Russell, entertained kids daily on NBC, beginning in October, 1950. The young viewers squealed with delight each time puppets El Squeeko Mouse, Gala Poochie and Polka Dottie put in their appearances on the show. Order was preserved in between movie cartoons by the Keystone Kops. The show lasted until November, 1952.

Host Todd Russell, Rootie Kazootie, Gala Poochie, Polka Dottie and a Keystone Kop of *The Rootie Kazootie Show.*

BROADWAY OPEN HOUSE

During the early 1950's one of the most popular late-night comedy-talk shows was *Broadway Open House*. It starred comedian Jerry Lester and featured a tall, curvaceous blonde with the suitably Scandinavian name of Dagmar. The forerunner of NBC's current late-night offering, *The Tonight Show*, Lester's late-late opus with its Beanbag Club and hilarious takeoffs of fairy tales, which featured big Dagmar as such unlikely characters as Little Red Riding Hood and Little Miss Muffet, convulsed audiences. Other regulars on the show included David Street, Wayne Howell and musical director and accordionist Milton Delugg.

Broadway Open House **star Jerry Lester is surrounded by regulars on the show.**

THE FRANK SINATRA SHOW

Singing star Frank Sinatra made his TV debut in a weekly half hour musical program on CBS in 1950. It ran for two years. Since 1952 Frank has turned to special shows and guest spots, appearing on *The Colgate Comedy Hour,* with Bing Crosby, and *The Chevy Show* with Dinah Shore.

Frank Sinatra, the star of his own show in 1952.

ARTHUR MURRAY'S DANCE PARTY

A popular program which was publicly recalled each time one network or another canceled it was *The Arthur Murray Dance Party*, which first appeared in 1950. Originally designed to give on-the-air dance instructions to at-home viewers (à la the Arthur Murray Dance Studios), a musical-variety show format eventually evolved. Kathryn Murray, Arthur's energetic and vivacious wife, was the real star of the show, with Arthur doing his duty as a straight man or dance partner. The Murrays managed to squeeze a nine-year run out of the series before retiring to Hawaii.

Kathryn and Arthur Murray.

YOUR HIT PARADE

In 1950 NBC dusted off its old *Hit Parade* radio show, which had been such a hit in the 1940's, and moved it to television as a summer replacement. By October sufficient public interest had been aroused to keep the show on as a permanent attraction. Eileen Wilson, Snooky Lanson and Dorothy Collins were the singing stars, and Raymond Scott provided the musical background. In 1952 June Valli replaced Miss Wilson, and Russell Arms joined her, Miss Collins and Mr. Lanson. Gisele MacKenzie replaced Miss Valli the following season. But by 1958 it was clear that rock-and-roll music was going to dominate the song popularity charts for a long time to come. Highly stylized, the songs were almost inseparable from the artists who made them famous. Since the "Hit Paraders" were not familiar with that kind of music and since some of the hit tunes remained in the top ten for weeks on end, novel ways of staging the songs became more difficult. In 1959 the "Lucky Strike Gang" swayed back and forth singing "So long for a while . . . that's all the songs for a while" for the last time.

Russell Arms (standing second from left), June Valli, Snooky Lanson, Dorothy Collins and Raymond Scott and the Lucky Strike Hit Parade Chorus sing "So long for a while . . . "

BEAT THE CLOCK

Once a week Bud Collyer led studio contestants through some pretty exhausting paces as they tried to beat the clock by performing close to impossible stunts. Mr. Collyer's beautiful blond assistant, Roxanne, who introduced the contestants to Mr. Collyer and the home viewers, became a TV celebrity in her own right.

MC Bud Collyer of *Beat the Clock.*

BIG TOP

The Big Top, a popular CBS circus show, made its television debut in 1950, with ringmaster Jack Sterling presiding. Clowns, high-wire acts and animals, as well as interviews with kids in the studio audience, were featured weekly. Mr. Sterling was assisted by clown Ed McMahon, who later became better known as Johnny Carson's *Tonight Show* sidekick. The program had a healthy seven-year run on CBS before blowing its circus whistle for the last time in September, 1957.

Ringmaster Jack Sterling and clown Ed McMahon of CBS' *The Big Top.*

BOB HOPE

Bob Hope's annual Christmas show with the boys overseas has been a TV ritual. He is seen here with Maria "The Body" McDonald during one of these shows.

America's favorite comedian.

America's favorite comedian, Bob Hope, made his television debut on *The Star Spangled Revue*, on NBC, in 1950. He's been seen regularly on TV ever since. He has starred in such shows as *The Chesterfield Sound-Off Time, The Colgate Comedy Hour* and a monthly *Bob Hope Show*. His Christmas shows with servicemen and women overseas and his Academy Award presentation appearances have been annual musts for millions of TV viewers.

The star of the legitimate theater's successful *Blackout* shows, Ken Murray had a CBS television show of his own from 1950 to 1952. A veteran showman and vaudevillian, Murray was one of the first performers to realize TV's potential for keeping vaudeville alive. His variety extravaganzas proved just the right thing to revive this dying form of entertainment. Ken's sidekick, a pretty, wide-eyed cowgirl named Laurie Anders, added to the *Murray Show* merriment.

Ken Murray and Laurie Anders.

SUPERMAN

"It's a bird . . . it's a plane . . . *it's Superman! The Adventures of Superman* enjoyed the same success on television it had in comic strips, on the radio and in motion pictures. George Reeves played the dual role of Clark Kent and Superman. Noel Neill was seen as Lois Lane, Jack Larson played teen-aged copyboy Jimmy, and John Hamilton *Daily Planet* newspaper editor in chief Perry White. The show first appeared on TV screens across the country as a syndicated series in 1950 and has been shown continuously ever since.

George Reeves as *Superman*.

1951

MACARTHUR RELIEVED OF KOREAN
COMMAND AFTER DEMANDING INVA-
SION OF RED CHINA . . . . ARMISTICE
TALKS BETWEEN UN AND KOREAN
COMMUNISTS BEGIN AT PANMUNJON
. . . . JAPANESE PEACE TREATY SIGNED
BY 49 NATIONS IN SAN FRANCISCO . . . .
ALGER HISS GOES TO PRISON FOR
PERJURY . . . .

ABBOTT AND COSTELLO

Bud Abbott and Lou Costello.

The comedy team of Bud Abbott and Lou Costello had a situation comedy series in the early 1950's after making several guest appearances on *The Colgate Comedy Hour*. The series, which featured variations of their "Who's on first?" comedy routine, also starred actress Hillary Brooke.

AMAHL AND THE NIGHT VISITORS

The Three Kings, played by Leon Lishner, Andrew McKinley and David Aiken, and Amahl's mother, played by Rosemary Kuhlman, in a scene from *Amahl and the Night Visitors.*

The first opera commissioned expressly for television, Gian Carlo Menotti's *Amahl and the Night Visitors*, was premiered on Christmas Eve, 1951. In this story of a crippled boy who plays host to the Three Kings on their way to pay tribute to the Christ Child in Bethlehem, Chet Allen appeared as the boy, Amahl, and Rosemary Kuhlman sang the role of his mother. Response to the show was so great that NBC made the opera an annual Christmas tradition.

THE ERNIE KOVACS SHOW

Comic genius Ernie Kovacs.

The bizarre, wildly original, zany comic talents of comedian Ernie Kovacs first began delighting TV audiences in 1951, when his show was televised from Philadelphia over the NBC national network. Ernie was the first comedian to realize the unique potentials TV held for comedians. His close-up direct conversations with the camera, his special camera effects, his Nairobi tribe of music-playing gorillas had audiences howling. And who could forget his Percy Dovetonsils, the nasal-sounding poet with eyeglasses as thick as a soda pop bottle? In 1955 Ernie's show included his wife, Edie Adams, who did brilliant takeoffs on actresses Marilyn Monroe and Zsa Zsa Gabor. Ernie's show was canceled in 1956, and thereafter he confined his television activities to occasional guest appearances and specials such as *Ernie in Kovacsland*. His career was cut tragically short when he was killed in an auto accident in 1962. His unique TV comic spirit has never been equaled.

Pianist Eddie Hatrak with Edie Adams and Ernie.

Zany Lucy cuts up with a more sober Desi Arnaz.

The Ricardos and the Mertzes found themselves in jail in this *I Lovy Lucy* episode. From left to right: guest Will Wright, Ricky (Desi), Ethel, Lucy, Fred, and Tennessee Ernie Ford.

I LOVE LUCY

The most successful situation comedy series in the history of television, *I Love Lucy*, starring Lucille Ball and Desi Arnaz, first saw the glow of TV success in 1951. The show revolved around bandleader Ricky Ricardo (Arnaz), his zany, trouble-prone wife, Lucy (Miss Ball), and their funny neighbors and friends Fred and Ethel Mertz, played by William Frawley and Vivian Vance. Loosely based on Miss Ball's hit radio show *My Favorite Husband* and retaining many of her original writers, the *Lucy* show quickly became a national institution. In 1952, when Miss Ball became pregnant, zealous TV officials decided to make Lucy Ricardo pregnant as well.

The birth of Lucy's TV baby, a boy who was called Little Ricky, made

Lucy Ball awaits the birth of her celebrated baby.

national headlines. In real life Miss Ball had had a baby girl. Following his divorce from Miss Ball, Mr. Arnaz retired from the series. The following year Lucy returned alone with a new format and show titled *The Lucille Ball Show*. During *I Love Lucy*'s heyday the Desilu Company initiated a one-hour dramatic series called *The Desilu Playhouse*, which also had a profitable run on TV.

Fred and Ethel Mertz were played by Vivian Vance and William Frawley.

THE SENATE CRIME HEARINGS

Frank Costello, an underworld character being questioned by the committee, refused to have his face telecast. The TV cameras therefore concentrated on his hands.

In March, 1951, television came into its own with in-depth, on-the-spot coverage of important news events. CBS and NBC simultaneously presented the U.S. Senate hearings on crime in America. All day long, viewers would sit fascinated in front of their TV sets as Senators Estes Kefauver and Charles Tobey and lawyer Rudolph Halley questioned such czars of the underworld as Frank Costello and ex-gangsters' moll Virginia Hill. Most of the witnesses pleaded the Fifth—"I refuse to answer on the grounds that it may tend to incriminate me"—a statement that became a household phrase in homes all over America. Because of the hearings, Americans were made frighteningly aware of how a national web of crime could touch their everyday lives.

AMOS 'N' ANDY

Amos, Andy, the Kingfish, Sapphire and all the funny folk of the popular *Amos 'n' Andy* radio show were transferred to television in 1951 with an all-black cast. The characters of Amos and Andy, originally played on radio by white actors Charles Correll and Freeman Gosden, were portrayed on TV by Spencer Williams (Andy) and Alvin Childress (Amos). The most popular character on the program remained the Kingfish, played by Tim Moore. The show was finally canceled from television in 1953, when the NAACP and other civil-rights groups protested the way the show pictured the American black man.

Spencer Williams and Alvin Childress as Amos and Andy.

JACKIE GLEASON

Jackie Gleason's first television show was called *The Cavalcade of Stars* and was broadcast over the New York local Dumont station. The program featured all of Jackie's famous TV characters—the Poor Soul, Reggie Van Gleason, Ralph Cramden and Joe the Bartender. Also appearing on the show were comedienne Pert Kelton and comic Larry Storch. In 1952 Gleason's national drawing power was put to the test. He gained instant fame across the country as star of a network variety-comedy series. One of the popular features of the Gleason show, the Honeymooners, proved so popular that a separate half hour situation comedy series was created from it.

"And away we go!"—Gleason's famous line.

"The Honeymooners"—Ralph Cramden (Gleason), his neighbor Ed Norton (Art Carney), his wife, Alice (Audrey Meadows), and Ed's wife, Trixie (Joyce Randolph).

The Goodyear Playhouse's *A Visit to a Small Planet*, presented in 1955, featured Louis Edmonds, Cyril Ritchard and Jill Kraft.

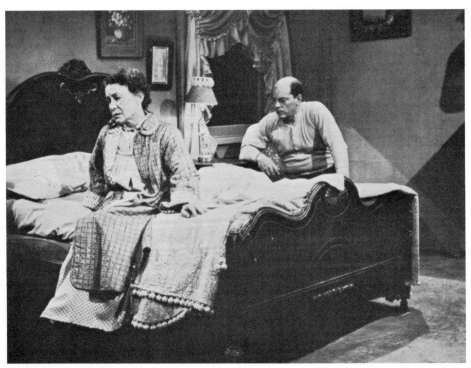

A successful motion picture was made of *The Catered Affair*, first seen on *The Goodyear Playhouse* in 1955. Thelma Ritter and Pat Henning starred in the television version of the play.

THE GOODYEAR PLAYHOUSE

Lillian Gish and Eva Marie Saint starred in *A Trip to Bountiful*, in 1953.

The Goodyear Playhouse dramatic series, produced by Fred Coe, was responsible for bringing some of television's most successful and celebrated plays before the public. Paddy Chayefsky's award-winning *Marty*, starring Rod Steiger in the title role, later would win an Academy Award for Ernest Borgnine when it was made into a major motion picture. *The Catered Affair*, with Thelma Ritter, was also made into a motion picture starring Bette Davis, and *The Bachelor Party* became yet another successful film. *The Goodyear Playhouse* was also the first to present *A Trip to Bountiful*, with Lillian Gish, and Gore Vidal's *A Visit to a Small Planet*, both of which were later made into Broadway stage plays. In 1957 the series became a half hour show and closed its curtain for the final time a short time later.

PINKY LEE SHOW

Lisping burlesque comedian Pinky Lee first appeared in the weekly musical-variety series *The Two of Us* with Vivian Blaine in 1951. The show ran for two years on NBC. In 1953 Pinky brought his baggy suit and funny hat to daytime TV, with a show designed for the kiddies. During one of these shows Pinky, while still "on the air," collapsed and thereafter retired from TV.

The Two of Us starred **Vivian Blaine and Pinky Lee.**

RACKET SQUAD

One weekly TV mystery-crime show which provided a public service, as well as entertainment, was CBS' *Racket Squad*. The series, which starred Reed Hadley as Detective Braddock of the Racket Squad, informed viewers of the workings of various confidence-game racketeers, alerting viewers to beware of charming strangers. Captain Braddock arrested his last con man in 1953, but the show can still be seen on local reruns.

Reed Hadley as Captain Braddock of *Racket Squad.*

MACY'S THANKSGIVING DAY PARADE

Thanksgiving just wouldn't be the same without a telecast of *Macy's Annual Thanksgiving Day Parade*. The huge balloons of Mickey Mouse, Popeye the Sailor Man and other well known cartoon characters have been ushering in the Christmas shopping season for television viewers since 1951. Such notable TV personalities as Arlene Francis, Dave Garroway, Douglas Edwards, Bess Myerson and Marilyn Van Derbur have acted as TV hosts for the *Parade* over the years.

Guest star Frank Sinatra and Dinah Shore of *The Chevy Show.*

RED SKELTON SHOW

Red Skelton as Freddie the Freeloader.

Indestructible comedian Red Skelton came to television from the movies and nightclubs in 1953. *The Red Skelton Show*, which is still a favorite, featured all of Red's crazy characterizations including Freddie the Freeloader, Willy Lump Lump, The Drunk, George Appleby, The Henpecked Husband, Clem Kaddidle-hoffer, Cookie the Sailor, Prizefighter Cauliflower McPugg, Deadeye the Cowboy and others. Red's pantomime routines earned him the much deserved title of the Marcel Marceau of Television. During Red's years on television he has had such famous guests as Marilyn Maxwell, Lucille Ball and Desi Arnaz, Pat O'Brien, Barbara Nichols, Lon Chaney, Jr., Janis Paige, Marie Windsor and Edward Everett Horton. His hour-long comedy series has endured longer than any other similar show on television.

LIFE WITH FATHER

The producer-director of radio's *Studio One* and *The Ford Theatre*, Fletcher Markle, added television to his list of credits when, in 1953, he produced and directed the *Life with Father* series. A situation comedy based on the long-running Broadway play of the same name, the series starred Leon Ames as Father and Lurene Tuttle as Mother shown left. The show also featured Ralph Reed, Freddie Leiston, Ronald Keith and Harvey Grant as their redheaded sons.

JOE FRANKLIN'S MEMORY LANE

Television's longest-reigning King of Nostalgia, Joe Franklin, made his television debut one Sunday night in 1953 with Author Fannie Hurst, his first TV guest. One of the few personality interviewers to broadcast successfully on both radio and TV simultaneously, Joe's "remember when" format has been a favorite with the viewing public for more than fifteen years and with the listening public even longer than that. In 1954 Joe moved from nighttime TV telecasting to the daytime, where he has been ever since. In 1958 Joe conducted a 90-minute in-depth interview with his idol, Eddie Cantor, which was presented free from commercial interruptions as a tribute to Eddie.

Singer Barbra Streisand, before stage and motion-picture fame, made one of her first appearances on TV on *The Joe Franklin Show*. Barbra (left) and Joe (right) flank physical culturist Jack Lalanne.

TWO FOR THE MONEY

The Hoosier Hotshot Herb Shriner was the host of the weekly half hour quiz show *Two for the Money* from 1953 to 1956. Contestants were asked questions for big money prizes and Dr. Mason Gross passed on the accuracy of their answers. Sam Levenson, the ex-schoolteacher, was a frequent substitute for Herb.

MC Herb Shriner asks contestants a question as Dr. Mason Gross looks on.

MARTY

Rod Steiger played Marty, Esther Minciotti his mother, and Betsy Palmer and Lee Phillips his sister-in-law and brother in *The Goodyear Playhouse*'s 1953 teleplay.

On May 24, 1953, *The Goodyear Playhouse* presented an original play by Paddy Chayefsky called *Marty*. The play, about a nearly middle-aged butcher who decides to break away from his Italian mother's apron strings and find a girlfriend of his own, made TV history. Directed by Delbert Mann and starring Rod Steiger, Nancy Marchand, Esther Minciotti, Betsy Palmer and Lee Phillips, the play was later made into an Academy Award-winning film which starred Ernest Borgnine.

WINKY DINK AND YOU

The real star of the *Winky Dink* children's show was a paper cutout character, although Jack Barry presided over the proceedings, announcing cartoons and encouraging the kids at home to join in the games, arts and crafts, and other projects being enjoyed by the kids in the studio audience. The show remained on CBS for four years.

Host Jack Barry, a young guest, and Winky Dink himself.

YOU ARE THERE

CBS' dean of newscasters Walter Cronkite hosted the *You Are There* series, which presented half hour recreations of historical events as if they were actually happening and being televised as on-the-spot news reports. The Boston Tea Party, the signing of the Declaration of Independence, the Battle of Verdun and the assassination of Julius Caesar were just a few of the events dramatized.

Walter Cronkite.

MEET MR. MC NULTY

Many Hollywood stars found their way to television in the early 1950's. One such was Ray Milland, who became the star of a weekly situation comedy series about a small-town schoolteacher, Mr. McNulty. The show, titled *Meet Mr. McNulty*, co-starred actress Phyllis Avery as Mr. Milland's wife.

Ray Milland as Mr. McNulty with guest star Miriam Hopkins.

MY FAVORITE HUSBAND

Lucille Ball's old radio show *My Favorite Husband* was dusted off and made into a TV series with Joan Caulfield playing Miss Ball's old role and Barry Nelson, of Broadway's *Moon Is Blue* fame, her husband. Vanessa Brown replaced Miss Caulfield after a few months, and the show ran until September, 1957.

My Favorite Husband stars Vanessa Brown and Barry Nelson with Sarah Selby, their maid.

PERSON TO PERSON

Veteran radio and TV newscaster Edward R. Murrow took viewers on visits to the homes of world celebrities on his weekly CBS *Person to Person* show. Using the TV monitor to talk to his guests, Murrow casually puffed on his cigarettes and asked probing questions of such notables as Marilyn Monroe, Louella Parsons, Mike Todd and his wife, Elizabeth Taylor, Marlon Brando, Jackie Robinson, the Duke and Duchess of Windsor, former President Harry S. Truman and Gypsy Rose Lee. When Murrow left the show in July, 1959, Charles Collingwood took over; but without Murrow the public soon lost interest, and the show left the air one year later.

Person to Person's **Edward R. Murrow.**

1954

RACIAL SEGREGATION IN PUBLIC SCHOOLS OUTLAWED BY U.S. SUPREME COURT . . . . DON LARSEN PITCHES PERFECT GAME; YANKEES LEAD BROOKLYN DODGERS IN WORLD SERIES . . . . CITATION WINS TRIPLE CROWN . . . . BEN HOGAN ADDS BRITISH OPEN TO HIS U.S. AND MASTERS GOLD TITLES . . . . U.S. SENATE VOTES TO CENSURE MCCARTHY FOR CONDUCT UNBECOMING A SENATOR . . . .

. . . and on TV . . .

THE ADVENTURES OF RIN TIN TIN

Set in the Golden West's favorite outpost, Fort Apache, *The Adventures of Rin Tin Tin* arrived on the TV scene in 1954. It starred youngster Lee Aaker as Rusty, an orphan adopted by the soldiers at the fort, James Brown as an Army officer and, of course, the famous German shepherd Rin Tin Tin (Rinny to his friends). For a while it looked as if Rinny might replace Lassie as America's favorite canine star, but when Lassie made her appearances on TV screens awhile later, Rinny had to take a second-place spot.

Rin Tin Tin, Lee Aaker and James Brown of *The Adventures of Rin Tin Tin* series.

THE SECRET STORM

The Secret Storm, a daytime viewing favorite of housewives all over America, was first seen on television in 1954. The series recorded the problems and triumphs of the Ames family. Other soap opera favorites, such as *As the World Turns, The Guiding Light* and *The Edge of Night*, have also enjoyed immense popularity with daytime viewers.

The Secret Storm cast: standing, Carl King as Bryan Fuller, Haila Stoddard as Pauline and Peter Hobbs as Peter Ames. Sitting are Marjorie Gateson as Mrs. Tyrrell and Beverly Lunsford as Amy Ames.

TENNESSEE ERNIE FORD SHOW

The king of the Southern pea pickers, Tennessee Ernie Ford, brought his deep voice and witty, if corny, country charm to television in 1954, when he starred on Kay Kyser's *Kollege of Musical Knowledge* show on NBC-TV. One year later, NBC officials rewarded him with a daytime show of his own which featured music, humor and pleasant chatter. His popularity increased, and in 1956 he starred in a prime-time evening variety hour. The show ran for four years on NBC.

Tennessee Ernie Ford's hymn singing was favorite finale of each telecast.

The Tennessee Ernie Ford show gang, from left to right, musical director Jack Fascinato, Skip Farrell, Doris Drew, Ernie, Molly Bee and Dick Williams.

STOP THE MUSIC

Bert Parks MC'd *Stop the Music* on television from 1954 to 1956. Each week the orchestra would play selections or vocalist Betty Ann Grove would sing a song until contestants chosen from the studio audience guessed the title. Parks sometimes relieved Miss Grove of the singing burden.

Stop the Music's **MC, Bert Parks.**

BLONDIE

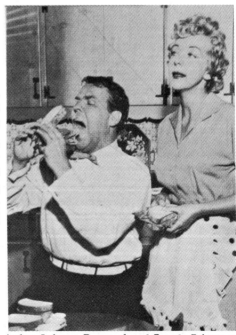

Chic Young's comic classic *Blondie*, which had been a motion-picture serial starring Penny Singleton as Blondie and Arthur Lake as Dagwood, was unsuccessfully made into a television series in 1954 with Mr. Lake playing his Dagwood role and Pamela Britton Blondie. The show lasted just one year. In the late 1960's NBC tried again but with even less success.

Arthur Lake as Dagwood and Pamela Britton as Blondie Bumstead.

ACADEMY AWARDS

The first telecast of the annual Academy Award presentations ran overtime, and William Holden, Oscar winner for his work in *Stalag 17* that year, was cut off in the middle of his acceptance speech. TV viewers had to turn to newspaper accounts the next morning to find that Audrey Hepburn had won an Oscar for her work in *Roman Holiday* and that the best movie of the year was judged to be *From Here to Eternity*.

Comedian Bob Hope has MC'd the Oscar shows fifteen times over the past years, and all three major networks have covered the events at one time or another.

The Academy of Motion Picture Arts & Sciences favorite MC, Bob Hope.

Before the Oscar telecasts.

NAME THAT TUNE

Music devotees could match their wits with studio contestants each week when George DeWitt asked them to try to identify popular song hits. The show, *Name That Tune*, which premiered in 1954, hit an all-time high on the Nielsen ratings when Eddie Hodges, the child star of Broadway's *Music Man*, appeared as a contestant on the show and bowled everyone over with his musical knowledge.

Name That Tune contestant Suzanne Saalsaa of Wisconsin is seen with her fiancé, Bill Zeimer, the show's host, George DeWitt, and contestant Mr. Lombardo.

THE MISS AMERICA CONTEST

The annual Miss America Contest telecast live from Atlantic City was first televised in 1954 with Bert Parks acting as MC. Many a contest winner has gone on to fame and fortune after being crowned Miss America.

In 1958 Marilyn Van Derbur was crowned Miss America. Bert Parks is seen serenading her with his now-familiar "There she is, Miss America . . . There she is, my ideal!"

FATHER KNOWS BEST

Millions of TV fans wouldn't miss a single episode of the delightful *Father Knows Best* situation-comedy series which starred easygoing, lovable Robert Young as "Father" Jim Anderson, Jane Wyatt as Mrs. Anderson (or Margaret, as Father called her), and Elinor Donahue, Billy Gray and Lauren Chapin as their children, Betty, Bud and Kathy. When CBS unwisely canceled the show after a mere two-year run in 1955, the public demanded its return, and it reappeared on NBC the following year. In 1958 it returned to its original home, CBS, where it remained to the early 1960's, when Father Young decided he had had enough. The show was noted for

Elinor Donahue, Lauren Chapin, Robert Young, Jane Wyatt and Billy Gray, the stars of *Father Knows Best.*

its natural presentation of the everyday problems of family living, and the Andersons were a model TV family for people all over America.

Son Bud, played by Billy Gray, with his parents, Jim and Margaret Anderson, played by Robert Young and Jane Wyatt.

THE MC CARTHY UN-AMERICAN
ACTIVITIES INVESTIGATIONS

The McCarthy Senatorial investigations into un-American activities became a daily and deadly household game for millions of viewers. Led by Senator Joseph McCarthy of Wisconsin, and supported by aides Private David Schine and lawyer Roy Cohn, the Senate subcommittee probed various branches of government—probably the most famous of which were the Army hearings at which distinguished lawyer Joseph Welch turned on McCarthy, saying: "Have you no sense of decency, sir? At long last, have you left no sense of decency?"

Roy Cohn confers with Senator Joseph McCarthy during the hearings.

LUX VIDEO THEATRE

In 1954, when TV was still showing films made mainly in the 1930's and early 1940's, *Lux Video Theatre* presented hour-long adaptations of recent films such as *To Each His Own, A Place in the Sun, Sunset Boulevard* and *Princess O'Rourke*. By 1957, however, television had begun to acquire an increasing number of recent films, and the need for TV adaptations diminished. Five years had been squeezed out of the *Lux Video Theatre* by the time it went off the air in 1957.

Diana Lynn and Ed Kemmer appeared in Lux's 1956 adaptation of the film *Princess O'Rourke*, which had originally starred Olivia De Havilland.

WALT DISNEY

In 1954 Walt Disney brought his special magic to television in a one-hour weekly series called *Disneyland*. Excerpts from some of Walt's popular films were presented, as well as adventure stories and nature films made especially for television. *Davy Crockett*, starring Fess Parker, was the show's most popular feature in the mid-1950's. In 1958 the show became *Walt Disney Presents*, and then in the 1960's its title was changed once again to Walt Disney's *Wonderful World of Color*.

Fess Parker as Davy Crockett, a popular feature on Walt Disney's *Disneyland* program which had thousands of youngsters sporting coonskin caps in mid-1950's.

Walt Disney and his friends
Mickey Mouse and Donald Duck.

SMILIN' ED

Ed McConnell was the host and storyteller of the popular daytime children's show *Smilin' Ed's Gang*. First seen in 1954, it ran for many seasons, keeping youngsters occupied while Mother did her household chores.

Smilin' Ed McConnell and his storybook.

THE BIG PAYOFF

Randy Merriman was the host and star of CBS' weekly *Big Payoff* quiz program, but it was his assistant, Bess Myerson, who received the most attention as she modeled the mink coat contestants could win along with a trip anywhere they desired.

Randy Merriman and Bess Myerson congratulate a winning couple.

PRIVATE SECRETARY

Ann Sothern, the movies' popular Maisie, became Susie McNamara, a private secretary, on this 1954 situation comedy series. Don Porter played her boss, Peter Sands, and Ann Tyrell Vi, a dim-witted office switchboard operator. In 1958 Miss Sothern changed identities, becoming Katy O'Connor, the assistant manager of a large hotel. Once again, Don Porter was her boss, this time as hotel owner Mr. Devery.

Ann Sothern as private secretary Susie McNamara.

Miss Sothern's 1958 series had her appearing as hotel assistant Katy O'Connor. Jack Mullaney played the bellboy, Johnny, and Jacques Scott hotel desk clerk, Paul.

DECEMBER BRIDE

The old mother-in-law jokes were expanded into a half hour situation comedy series when CBS presented character actress Spring Byington as mother-in-law Lily Ruskin in a show called *December Bride*. This "joke" was different, however, in that Lily Ruskin wasn't a mean old nasty lady but a sweet and dear old thing, deeply loved by her family and friends. Miss Byington was given able support by Frances Rafferty and Dean Miller as her daughter and son-in-law, Ruth and Matt Henshaw, and Henry Morgan and Verna Felton as friends and neighbors, Pete and Hilda.

The *December Bride* cast—sitting: Frances Rafferty, Spring Byington and Dean Miller; standing, Verna Felton and Henry Morgan.

MY FRIEND IRMA

Radio's dumb blonde Irma Peterson, played by Marie Wilson, was made into a television heroine in 1954 with Miss Wilson and Cathy Lewis recreating their radio roles for the television cameras. Miss Lewis was replaced shortly after the show went on the air by Mary Shipp as Jane.

Marie Wilson, Paul Frees and Mary Shipp on a *My Friend Irma* show in 1954.

1955

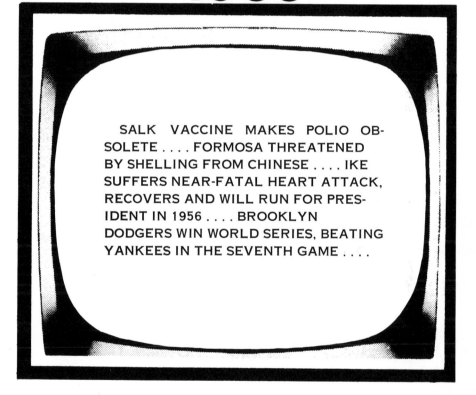

SALK VACCINE MAKES POLIO OB-
SOLETE . . . . FORMOSA THREATENED
BY SHELLING FROM CHINESE . . . . IKE
SUFFERS NEAR-FATAL HEART ATTACK,
RECOVERS AND WILL RUN FOR PRES-
IDENT IN 1956 . . . . BROOKLYN
DODGERS WIN WORLD SERIES, BEATING
YANKEES IN THE SEVENTH GAME . . . .

and our entertainment . . .

THE RIFLEMAN

With his Winchester rifle under one arm and his motherless son under the other, the Rifleman, Lucas McCain, played by tall ex-baseball star Chuck Connors, battled evil on his ABC weekly Western series. From the first broadcast in 1955, *The Rifleman* became the country's most popular Western show.

Chuck Connors, former baseball star and TV's Rifleman.

YOU'LL NEVER GET RICH

One of the rare instances in which the main character of a series became better known than the title of the show was *You'll Never Get Rich* which featured Sergeant Ernest G. Bilko as played by comedian Phil Silvers. Bilko, a fast-talking Army sergeant with a million get-rich-quick schemes, was the star of a favorite fun-filled half hour. With his sidekicks, Paul Ford as Colonel Hall and Allan Melvin and Harvey Lembeck as members of his platoon, Bilko talked his way in and out of hundreds of seemingly impossible situations before ending his mouth marathon in 1959.

George Matthews and Phil Silvers as Sergeant Bilko.

Bilko (center) conning members of his platoon.

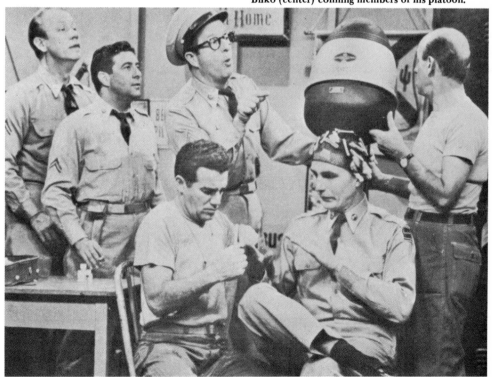

THE ADVENTURES OF ROBIN HOOD

TV's Robin Hood, Richard Greene.

Robin Hood, Robin Hood,
Riding through the glen.
Robin Hood, Robin Hood,
With his band of men.
Feared by the bad,
Loved by the good,
Robin Hood! Robin Hood! Robin Hood!

The above theme song introduced the British made TV series *The Adventures of Robin Hood* to listening audiences each week. The show starred former movie star Richard Greene as Robin.

ALFRED HITCHCOCK PRESENTS

Alfred Hitchcock presenting . . . .

Movieland's master of mystery Alfred Hitchcock produced a TV series of cliff-hanging tales over the CBS network in 1955 which ran for more than eight years. The half hour series called *Alfred Hitchcock Presents* had Mr. Hitchcock on hand to introduce and close each telecast. Although it sometimes seemed as if criminals might go unpunished at the end of the show, Mr. Hitchcock would always assure his audience that some sort of justice would prevail in the end.

PETER PAN

Cyril Ritchard.

Mary Martin.

An oft-repeated TV special, *Peter Pan*, a musical adventure which starred musical comedy star Mary Martin as Peter and featured Cyril Ritchard as Captain Hook, was first telecast on March 7, 1955. Well-known Broadway choreographer Jerome Robbins staged this television musical adaptation of James M. Barrie's classic tale of a boy who never grew up. Such songs as "Never, Never Land," "I Gotta Crow," "I'm Flying," and "Never Smile at a Crocodile" became Tin Pan Alley favorites. The special was so popular NBC repeated it months after its first showing and several times thereafter.

KRAFT MUSIC HALL

The former star of *The Chesterfield Supper Club*, Perry Como, switched from selling cigarettes to cheese when he became the star of *The Kraft Music Hall* show on NBC. Mitchell Ayres and his orchestra and the Ray Charles Singers provided the musical background for Perry's singing, and announcer Frank Gallop introduced the show.

The end of a Perry Como *Kraft Music Hall* show finds Perry surrounded by guests, comic Bert Lahr, singer Kay Starr, Perry, actress Anne Bancroft and the popular Mills Brothers.

135

"Champagne Lady" Alice Lon and Lawrence Welk
dance the polka.

LAWRENCE WELK SHOW

Bandleader Lawrence Welk and his champagne music arrived on TV as a summer replacement show in 1955. The public decided it liked what it saw, and Welk was given a regular show and has been fast stepping on television screens across America ever since. With Alice Lon, his first Champagne Lady, who left the show in the late 1950's, singers Dick Dale, the Lennon Sisters, Larry Hooper, Jerry Burke, Tiny Little, Jr., Joanne Castle and Joe Feeney, to mention a few, the old machine has been blowing bubbles across TV screens for more than fifteen years.

The popular Lennon Sisters, Dianne, Peggy, Kathy and Janet.

THE ADVENTURES OF SIR LANCELOT

NBC imported the British television series *The Adventures of Sir Lancelot* in 1955 and aimed it at the young TV viewing audience. The series starred England's William Russell as Sir Lancelot and had a two-year stay on NBC. In 1957 it moved to the ABC network, where it remained for one more year.

Garry Thorne and Sir Lancelot, William Russell, fight a duel on *The Adventures of Sir Lancelot.*

SGT. PRESTON OF THE YUKON

The Canadian Mounted Police took to the television airwaves in 1955 in a syndicated show, *Sgt. Preston of the Yukon*, which starred Richard Simmons as the daring Mountie Sergeant Preston and featured his horse, Rex, and his dog, Yukon King.

Sgt. Preston of the Yukon **(Richard Simmons), his horse, Rex, and his dog, Yukon King.**

THE JOHNNY CARSON SHOW

Long before his success as the master of ceremonies on NBC's *Tonight Show*, Johnny Carson was the star of a weekly situation comedy series over the CBS network called *The Johnny Carson Show*. Prior to this less than successful series, Johnny had made a hit as a guest star on such variety shows as Ed Sullivan's *Toast of the Town* and *The Colgate Comedy Hour*.

Johnny Carson and Glenn Turnbull on CBS' 1955 situation comedy series *The Johnny Carson Show.*

MIKE WALLACE INTERVIEWS

Frank, sometimes shocking questions were TV interviewer Mike Wallace's stock-in-trade. Wallace probed into the lives of such celebrities as Diana Barrymore, playwright Tennessee Williams, architect Frank Lloyd Wright and radio interviewer Mary Margaret McBride. Because of Wallace's soul-searching questions, many a lawsuit was filed once subjects realized just how much of themselves Wallace had caused them to reveal on the show.

Ace interviewer Mike Wallace.

WIDE WIDE WORLD

NBC presented veteran TV performer Dave Garroway in a news-interview program, *Wide Wide World*, in 1955. Some of Dave's guests included comedian Milton Berle and singer Perry Como. It remained on NBC for three years.

Wide Wide World's host, Dave Garroway.

PATTERNS

Writer Rod Serling's masterpiece, *Patterns*, a TV play about the shady dealings in the world of big business, was presented on *The Kraft Theatre* in 1955. The TV play starred Richard Kiley as a disillusioned young business executive, Ed Begley as an older executive about to be put to pasture and Everett Sloane as the cruel and ruthless head of the corporation. Four weeks after it was originally presented on *Kraft*, it was repeated by popular request. The play, directed by Fielder Cook, was later made into a motion picture with the entire TV cast intact.

Ed Begley, Everett Sloane and Richard Kiley in *The Kraft Theatre* **presentation of Rod Serling's** *Patterns.*

BIL AND CORA BAIRD

Marionettists Bil and Cora Baird had many shows on television, but their most popular was CBS' *The Morning Show* which starred Walter Cronkite. The Bairds' chief function on the AM offering was to occupy the kids who were too young to be in school while Mother temporarily left Mr. Cronkite to clean up the breakfast dishes.

Cora and Bil Baird and their marionettes.

THE U.S. STEEL HOUR

The Theatre Guild, with United States Steel as its sponsor, produced a series of hour-long television plays starting in 1955. *The Meanest Man in the World* was the first offering, and over the years the show presented such plays as *Hidden River, Midsummer, Upbeat* and the original production of *No Time for Sergeants* starring Andy Griffith, before it was made into a successful Broadway play and motion picture. Some of the stars to appear on the *Steel Hour* were Helen Hayes, Richard Kiley, Martyn Green, Patty Duke and William Shatner.

Andy Griffith in *No Time for Sergeants* on *The U.S. Steel Hour,* prior to the stage and motion-picture productions.

Robert Culp, later the star of *I Spy,* and heiress Gloria Vanderbilt played young lovers in *U.S. Steel's* production of *Flint and Fire.*

THE JUDY GARLAND SPECIAL

On September 24, 1955, Movieland's Judy Garland made her long-awaited TV debut on a special on the CBS network singing all the songs that had made her famous. The show, called *The Ford Star Jubilee*, received the highest ratings recorded up to that time, and Judy was in demand as a TV performer thereafter. She preferred, however, to keep her TV appearances to a minimum, and not until several years later did viewers see Judy again on their TV's.

Judy Garland and her guest star, David Wayne, on *The Ford Star Jubilee.*

PEOPLE'S CHOICE

Former child movie star Jackie Cooper became a television star on NBC's *People's Choice*. The appealing Mr. Cooper had the show stolen away from him each week by basset hound Cleo. Cooper played a civil servant who lived in a trailer with his pet and worked his way in and out of trouble with the aid of his girlfriend, played by Patricia Breslin. The show ran for three years on NBC and then moved to ABC in 1959 for several more seasons before calling it quits in the early 1960's.

Jackie Cooper, Cleo, the basset hound, and Patricia Breslin of *People's Choice.*

GUNSMOKE

CBS' durable *Gunsmoke* series made its TV debut in 1955, and the weekly adventure is still running strong on that network. The stars of the show, James Arness as Marshal Matt Dillon, Amanda Blake as the saloonkeeping Kitty, Milburn Stone as Doc and Dennis Weaver as Chester became famous through their association with the show, record sales, personal appearances at country fairs, a weekly radio show and perpetual reruns. Even when the popular, limping Chester (Dennis Weaver) decided to leave the show in the late 1950's, its popularity did not diminish, and Kitty's "Be careful, Matt" and Chester's "Well, I dunno, Meester Dellon" have become household expressions.

Dodge City's Marshal Matt Dillon, played by James Arness.

Kitty, played by Amanda Blake, and Matt, played by James Arness of *Gunsmoke*.

WYATT EARP

The celebrated marshal of Tombstone, Wyatt Earp, was the hero of a popular TV Western series which starred handsome Hugh O'Brian in 1955. One of television's best-remembered Western hits, the show enjoyed a long run.

Hugh O'Brian as Tombstone Marshal Wyatt Earp.

THE BOB CUMMINGS SHOW

Bob Cummings, Rosemary De Camp and Hans Conried surround Ann B. Davis, Schultzy of *The Bob Cummings Show.*

In 1955 Bob Cummings, who had starred in the *My Hero* situation comedy series several seasons before, had a new show on the air, called *The Bob Cummings Show.* On the new series Bob played a bachelor photographer, Bob Collins. Rosemary De Camp, whose voice was familiar to listeners as Judy on the past popular *Dr. Christian* radio program, played Bob's sister, Rosemary, and Dwayne Hickman, who later became better known as TV's Dobie Gillis, played his nephew, Chuck. Much of the show's humor, however, was provided by Ann B. Davis as Bob's secretary, Schultzy, a man-hungry spinster who never gave up hope that Bob someday would be hers. When the show went off the air in 1957, Bob still wasn't hers or anybody else's, but still a gay and carefree bachelor.

OUR TOWN

Frank Sinatra, as *Our Town*'s stage manager.

The Producer's Showcase special *Our Town*, a musical adaptation of Thornton Wilder's classic stage play, starred three of Hollywood's most popular stars, Frank Sinatra as the stage manager-narrator, Paul Newman and Eva Marie Saint. The show provided TV with its first hit song, "Love and Marriage," which was sung on the show by Frank.

Paul Newman and Eva Marie Saint played the young lovers on *The Producer's Showcase* production of *Our Town*.

CAPTAIN KANGAROO

Children took special delight in the soft-spoken antics of a mustached, gray-headed "former sea captain," Captain Kangaroo, who in reality was a young actor named Bob Keeshan. The captain's gentle conversation, charming fantasy sense and fun-filled arts and crafts activities were directed at the preschool youngsters by Mr. Keeshan, who had played Clarabel the Clown on the popular *Howdy Doody* show for many years before becoming Captain Kangaroo. The show received many awards from PTA groups and educators all over the country.

Bob Keeshan was TV's Captain Kangaroo for six years.

THE MILLIONAIRE

Michael Anthony, played by Marvin Miller, hands over a million-dollar check from "John Beresford Tipton."

"Michael, I have another check for you to deliver," TV's fictitious billionaire John Beresford Tipton told his executive secretary, Michael Anthony, each week on *The Millionaire* series, and millions of viewers wished they were the ones lucky enough to get that check. Anthony, played by actor Marvin Miller, presented the checks to different recipients, telling them: "I have here a certified cashier's check for one million dollars tax-exempt, made out in your name from a benefactor who wishes to remain anonymous. Should you reveal where you got this check to anyone but your wife, if you are married, you must return the unused portion." By the time this dramatic anthology series left the air, Mr. Tipton was poorer by about $70,000,000.

$64,000 QUESTION

The late Hal March was brought to national attention as the star of one of TV's most successful quiz programs, *The $64,000 Question*, television's flamboyant version of radio's modest *$64 Question*. Viewers were awed by the sums involved, and the show was lavish in every respect. Experts on fields ranging from boxing to grand opera were asked questions which became increasingly more difficult. A contestant kept doubling his winnings each time he answered correctly, but he could quit at any point and keep his winnings. Home and studio audiences alike got frantic either urging contestants to keep trying—or stop at their present "plateau." Shoemaker

Hal March is surrounded by winning contestants on *The $64,000 Question* show.

Gino Prato, the opera buff, Dr. Joyce Brothers, the psychologist whose forte was boxing, Robert Strom, the mathematics genius, and actor Vincent Price, the art expert, were just a few of the many big money winners. The program was so popular that a second show, a sequel called *The $64,000 Challenge*, MC'd by Sonny Fox, was also offered. The TV quiz show scandal about "fixed" questions, which mainly concerned the *Twenty-One* program, made the public question the honesty of all the quiz programs, and soon after the scandal most of the big money giveaway programs, including *The $64,000 Question* and *Challenge*, left the air.

The host of *The $64,000 Question,* Hal March.

MICKEY MOUSE CLUB

Theme Song:
Who's the leader of the club
that's made for you and me?
M*I*C*K*E*Y M*O*U*S*E.
Mickey Mouse! Mickey Mouse!
Forever let us hold our banner
high! High! High!
Now it's time to sing along and
join our jamboree!
M*I*C*K*E*Y M*O*U*S*E!

Walt Disney and his Mickey Mouseketeers.

Everyone's favorite Walt Disney cartoon character Mickey Mouse became the star of a daily TV show for kids which was presented each afternoon just after school. Regular members of the Mousketeer Club—Bobby, Annette, Moochie, Linda, Cheryl, Karen, Doreen, Sharon and the rest—with Jimmy Dodd as their clubmaster, sang, danced and flapped their mousketeer-capped ears, and the whole menagerie of Disney cartoon characters, Pluto, Goofy, Donald Duck, Minnie Mouse, Daisy *et al*, joined in the fun, which featured Disney cartoons, live action serials like the popular *Spin and Marty* adventures and stories and games.

Closing Theme:
Now it's time to say good-bye to
all our company
M*I*C . . .
See you real soon.
K*E*Y . . .
Why? Because we love you!
M*O*U*S*E
Good-bye!

LASSIE

Ever since Metro-Goldwyn-Mayer first presented its screen adaptations of the famous Albert Payson Terhune *Lassie* stories, the collie had been everybody's favorite. When Lassie finally became a TV series in 1955, she had the field to herself with the possible exception of German shepherd Rin Tin Tin.

On the series, farm dog Lassie was owned by a young lad named Jeff, played by Tommy Rettig. Jeff's mother, a widow, was played by Broadway musical comedy star Jan Clayton, and Grandpa by George Cleveland. When Master Rettig became too old for dogs, he was replaced as Lassie's owner by young Jon Provost. Miss Clayton was replaced also by June Lockhart and Hugh Riley as Jon's parents. Since then, Lassie has had several owners, among them forest ranger Corey Stuart, played by Robert Bray.

Jon Provost, June Lockhart and Hugh Riley later became Lassie's owners.

Lassie's first TV family included Tommy Rettig, George Cleveland and Jan Clayton.

Shari Lewis

Betty Furness for Westinghouse

Violinist Florian ZaBachs

TV artist Jon Gnagy

TV PERSONALITIES

Interesting new faces were constantly appearing on television screens, and some, belonging to weather forecasters, pitchmen, guest stars and cooks, became as well known to viewers as the stars of the big shows.

Joyce Brothers

TV hostess Wendy Barrie

Pianist Van Cliburn

Mind reader Dunninger

Weatherman Tex Antoine and Uncle Wethbee

Soupy Sales

Betty White

Horror show host Zacherly

"The Continental" Renzo Cesano

Singer Kyle MacDonnell

Liberace

1956

EISENHOWER REELECTED PRESI-
DENT OF THE UNITED STATES . . . . HUN-
GARIANS REVOLT AGAINST RUSSIAN
OCCUPATION . . . . BRITISH SEIZE THE
SUEZ CANAL . . . . REPUBLICANS EN-
DORSE IKE AND DICK . . . . ISRAEL IN-
VADES SINAI PENINSULA IN RETALIA-
TION FOR EGYPTIAN ATTACKS . . . . U.S.
DEFENSES FALL BEHIND RUSSIA . . . .
SENATE SUBCOMMITTEE URGES
STRENGTHENING COUNTRY'S RETALIA-
TORY AIR POWER . . . .

In 1958 *Playhouse 90* presented **Geraldine Page** and **Tab Hunter** in *Portrait of a Murderer.*

Gladys Cooper and Rod Taylor in *Verdict of Three.*

Melvyn Douglas as Stalin in *Playhouse 90*'s *Plot to Kill Stalin* in 1958.

PLAYHOUSE 90

Television's first ninety-minute dramatic series made its auspicious debut on CBS in 1956, when *Playhouse 90* presented Rod Serling's *Forbidden Games*, with Charlton Heston and Tab Hunter playing the lead roles. During the years the show was on the air it presented such magnificent plays as *Requiem for a Heavyweight* starring Jack Palance and Ed Wynn; *For Whom the Bell Tolls* with Maria Schell, Jason Robards, Jr., Maureen Stapleton and Eli Wallach; *The Plot to Kill Stalin* with Melvyn Douglas; *The Helen Morgan Story* with Polly Bergen; and Kay Thompson's *Eloise*.

The Helen Morgan Story starred actress Polly Bergen as the tragic chanteuse.

Sterling Hayden and Geraldine Page appeared in the *Playhouse 90* adaptation of William Faulkner's *Old Man*.

Jason Robards, Jr., and Maria Schell were the stars of the 1959 *Playhouse 90* presentation of Ernest Hemingway's *For Whom the Bell Tolls*.

TRUTH OR CONSEQUENCES

When radio's *Truth or Consequences* came to television in 1956, gagster Ralph Edwards, who had starred on the radio version of the show for many years, also appeared in the TV version. When Mr. Edwards left the show to star on his *This Is Your Life* series, he was replaced by Bob Barker, who can still be seen leading *Truth or Consequences* guests through some pretty grueling paces each week.

Truth or Consequences **MC, Bob Barker.**

THE PRICE IS RIGHT

Bill Cullen was the host of the popular daytime *Price Is Right* series, which had contestants trying to guess the prices of various items of merchandise. The contestant guessing the price closest to the manufacturer's retail price received the prize. In 1957, because of the show's appeal, it was given a nighttime slot, with Mr. Cullen continuing as MC.

Bill Cullen (left) of TV's popular *The Price Is Right.*

TO TELL THE TRUTH

TV producers Goodson and Todman, the leading forces behind most of TV's successful panel-game shows, presented *To Tell the Truth* as a daytime show in 1956. Its popularity with viewers led to an evening version of the show which featured at one time or another, panelists Tom Poston, Kitty Carlisle, Orson Bean, Polly Bergen, Peggy Cass, Ralph Bellamy and Hy Gardner.

Bud Collyer, the MC of CBS' *To Tell the Truth*, asks panel of Polly Bergen, Ralph Bellamy, Kitty Carlisle and Hy Gardner, to try to tell which of the three ladies on the platform is telling the truth about her identity.

TWENTY-ONE

The most successful, notorious and generous of the big-money giveaway programs was Jack Barry's *Twenty-One* series. Contestants on the show could win as much as $216,000 on the show, for there was no limit on the amount up for grabs. One of the show's biggest money winners was Charles Van Doren, who became a TV celebrity because of his appearances on the show. In 1958 the program left the air after the story broke that contestants had been given correct answers by the producers in order to make the show more interesting. This scandal was the beginning of the end for the TV big-money shows.

Twenty-One's host, Jack Barry. Behind him contestants Vivienne Nearing and Charles Van Doren wait in their isolation booths for their questions.

QUEEN FOR A DAY

Each weekday MC Jack Baily gave those at home a chance to become *Queen for a Day* vicariously as he interviewed typical American housewives in his studio audience and asked the audience to help him decide which of them should be crowned "Queen."

Nurse Julia Erich, a hopeful competitor for *Queen for a Day*, is seen being interviewed by MC Jack Baily.

CHEYENNE

Clint Walker as Cheyenne.

Tall, silent frontier scout, Cheyenne Brody, played by Clint Walker, loped his way across TV screens for the first time in 1956, when he became, for that year, at least, TV's undisputed Western champion. After a few short years *Cheyenne* suddenly disappeared from the airwaves because, it was later discovered, Mr. Walker had insisted on a larger salary. Angry fans demanded he be given his money, and the show reinstated. It was.

AMERICAN BANDSTAND

Teen-agers had a favorite TV show of their own in Dick Clark's afternoon *American Bandstand* program. Teens could dance to the tunes of the latest rock-and-roll recording hits, as well as be entertained by guests like Fabian, Little Anthony, Frankie Avalon and Chubby Checkers, who made frequent appearances on the show. Beginning as a local show in Philadelphia in 1955, it graduated to network broadcasting the following year. In 1958 ABC presented an evening version, but it proved less popular than in its afternoon spot, to which, after a few months, Clark moved the show.

Dick Clark, the host of the *American Bandstand*, with studio audience of teens.

THE BOING BOING SHOW

Gerald McBoing Boing of *The Boing Boing Show.*

The popular CBS children's cartoon program, *The Boing Boing Show*, featured cartoon character Gerald McBoing Boing, and was seen on the CBS network from December, 1956, to October, 1958.

REQUIEM FOR A HEAVYWEIGHT

The second play presented by CBS on its *Playhouse 90* series was a block-busting success. Playwright Rod Serling had already established himself as one of television's foremost writers, but with *Requiem for a Heavyweight*, which starred Jack Palance, Kim Stanley and Ed Wynn, he stepped way out in front as TV's leading writer. The play, which was about a prize-fighter named Mountain McClintock, showed the seamier side of the boxing world and won for *Playhouse 90* and its author several TV awards in 1956. The play was later made into a film with less success than it had enjoyed as a TV play.

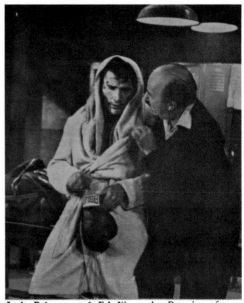

Jack Palance and Ed Wynn in *Requiem for a Heavyweight*.

TALES OF WELLS FARGO

The Wells Fargo organization was the Old West's only link with the civilized world during the 1800's, and NBC decided the adventures of Wells Fargo troubleshooters and stagecoach drivers would make a pretty snappy TV series. They proved right. Dale Robertson played troubleshooting Jim Hardie, who kept those stages rolling well into the late 1950's.

Tales of Wells Fargo featured Dale Robertson as troubleshooter Jim Hardie.

1957

EUROPEAN NATIONS FORM COMMON MARKET . . . . GOVERNOR FAUBUS OF ARKANSAS DEFIES SUPREME COURT DESEGREGATION ORDER. NEGROES DENIED ENTRY INTO ARKANSAS SCHOOLS . . . . U.S. GOVERNMENT SENDS FEDERAL TROOPS TO LITTLE ROCK . . . . SOVIETS LAUNCH SPUTNIK I MOON SATELLITE . . . . U.S. LAUNCHES EX-PLORER I, THE ARMY JUPITER ROCKET IN JANUARY . . . . NATION MOVES TO-WARD RECESSION, THE WORST IN RE-CENT YEARS . . . . CONGRESS PASSES TEMPORARY UNEMPLOYMENT COMPEN-SATION ACT . . . .

. . . and in spite of the headlines . . .

Robert Horton played Flint Mc-Cullough and Ward Bond Major Seth Adams in the *Wagon Train* series, which premiered in 1957. In 1961, after Mr. Bond died, he was replaced by veteran character actor John McIntyre as the wagon train's wagon master. Shortly thereafter, Horton decided to leave the series and was replaced first by Scott Miller and then by Robert Fuller. The show survived all these changes in cast and remained on the air until the mid-1960's.

Robert Horton, Carolyn Jones and Ward Bond are seen in a scene from *Wagon Train.*

ANDY'S GANG

Gravel-voiced movie and radio comedian Andy Devine was the host of a daily children's show called *Andy's Gang* in 1957. Young fans eagerly looked forward to the daily cartoons, clubhouse meetings and regular visits by Gunga Ram, the Elephant Boy, who was played by actor Nino Marcel and looked remarkably like the movies' Sabu.

Andy Devine and Gunga Ram (Nino Marcel) on *Andy's Gang.*

PERRY MASON

When Erle Stanley Gardner's famed lawyer Perry Mason came to television in 1957, fresh from a lengthy run as a radio daytime serial, he was played by veteran movie badman Raymond Burr in his first sympathetic role. Each week Perry, aided by his faithful secretary, Della Street, played by Barbara Hale, and his assistant, Paul Drake, played by William Hopper, set about to prove the innocence of his clients. Perry never lost a case in spite of the skillful maneuvers of his adversary, District Attorney Hamilton Burger, played by William Talman. *The Perry Mason Show* ran for nine years on television before Mr. Burr decided that it was time to change his image once again and appeared as the hero of *Ironsides*.

Raymond Burr as Perry Mason.

Perry Mason (Raymond Burr) and Della Street (Barbara Hale) seem to be in a difficult situation in this *Perry Mason* episode.

RICHARD DIAMOND PRIVATE DETECTIVE

Long before he began running from the law as TV's *Fugitive*, David Janssen played Richard Diamond, a private detective on the right side of the law, with a penchant for getting into trouble. The CBS series was seen from 1957 to 1959.

David Janssen, as *Richard Diamond, Private Detective*, protects guest Phyllis Kirk.

RESTLESS GUN

Movie star John Payne had a Western series called *Restless Gun* on NBC in 1957. The series was about the foreman of a ranch out West in the late 1800's.

John Payne of *Restless Gun* corners bad guy Chuck Connors.

THE PAT BOONE SHOW

Former Arthur Godfrey *Talent Scouts* winner Pat Boone was given a show of his own in 1957. Pat's white buck shoes and his easygoing college boy charm earned him a faithful TV following. Some of the big names who made guest appearances on Pat's show were Andy Williams (later a star in his own right), the Crosby Brothers (Bing's sons) and Peggy Lee.

Guest star Frankie Avalon exhibits his skill with a trumpet as Pat sings along on *The Pat Boone Show*.

164

THE SENATE RACKETS COMMITTEE
INVESTIGATIONS

Counsel Robert Kennedy, a young New York lawyer, Senator John Mc-Clellan and Senator John F. Kennedy became TV stars in 1957 when television covered the U.S. Senate investigations into rackets in America. For weeks millions of viewers watched as Bobby Kennedy hammered away at underworld characters like "Johnny Dio" Dioguardo, "Tony Ducks" Corallo, Joey Glimco and "Caesar" Di Varco, as well as union leaders like the Teamsters' Jimmy Hoffa and Dave Beck, who constantly "took the Fifth." The Senate committee meetings, which sought possible connections between unions and organized crime, brought considerable fame to the Kennedy brothers.

HAVE GUN WILL TRAVEL

In 1957 a literate, debonair Western hero named Paladin made his first appearance on TV in a CBS series called *Have Gun Will Travel.* Richard Boone as Paladin became a star overnight. Few viewers will forget Paladin's calling card which read: "Have gun will travel. Wire Paladin. Hotel Carlton, San Francisco."

Richard Boone as Paladin on *Have Gun Will Travel.*

LEAVE IT TO BEAVER

The mischievous life of a typical American boy was realistically reproduced each week on CBS' *Leave It to Beaver* series. Jerry Matthews played Beaver, and Tony Dow appeared as his big brother, Wally. The show proved very popular with adults who could identify with the problems faced by Beaver's parents.

Beaver, played by Jerry Matthews, and his parents, played by Barbara Billingsley and Hugh Beaumont.

MAVERICK

A new kind of Western hero made his appearance on television when ABC presented Maverick, the weekly adventures of a cowardly gambler-rogue played by handsome James Garner. Bret Maverick didn't ride a horse, loathed the out-of-doors, was slow on the draw and preferred sitting around gambling in musty, smoke-filled saloons. He was a very untypical Western hero indeed. Once the series had been established, a second unlikely hero made his appearance—Bret Maverick's brother, Bart, played by Jack Kelly.

Brother Bart Maverick was played by Jack Kelly.

James Garner is Bret Maverick.

The TV adaptation of *Billy Budd* presented by *Du Pont* starred James Donald, Don Murray and Roddy McDowall.

British stars Margaret Leighton and John Gielgud appeared in *The Browning Version* in 1959.

Mark Twain's *The Prince and the Pauper*, presented in 1957, starred Rosemary Harris, Christopher Plummer and Rex Thompson.

DU PONT SHOW OF THE MONTH

With a play called *Crescendo*, starring the unlikely team of Carol Channing and Mahalia Jackson, CBS initiated its monthly *Du Pont Show of the Month* series. Produced by David Susskind, the show presented such works as *The Bridge of San Luis Rey* with Judith Anderson, Hume Cronyn and Vivica Lindfors, *Billy Budd, The Browning Version* with Margaret Leighton and John Gielgud, *A Tale of Two Cities* with Eric Portman and Gracie Fields, *Hamlet* with John Neville, *The Count of Monte Cristo* with Hurd Hatfield, *A Member of the Wedding* with Claudia McNeil and Collin Wilcox and *Wuthering Heights* with Richard Burton.

Lee J. Cobb starred as Don Quixote for the *Du Pont Show of the Month.*

The Member of the Wedding starred Claudia McNeil, Collin Wilcox and Dennis Kohler.

Richard Burton and Yvonne Furneaux starred in *Wuthering Heights,* a 1958 *Du Pont Show of the Month.*

ZORRO

Guy Williams, as the masked Zorro, holds villain Charles Korvin at bay.

The adventure series *Zorro*, starring Guy Williams as the black-caped and masked "Robin Hood" of Mexico, had a two-year residency on ABC-TV beginning in 1957. Zorro's blade felled many a villain before he retired in 1959.

CINDERELLA

The famous Broadway musical comedy team of Richard Rodgers and Oscar Hammerstein II, the authors of such formidable hits as *Oklahoma, Carousel, The King and I* and *The Sound of Music*, wrote a musical adaptation of the children's classic fairy tale *Cinderella* especially for television. The show, first seen on March 31, 1957, and repeated with a new cast several seasons later, starred the *My Fair Lady* sensation Julie Andrews as Cinderella and featured Ilka Chase as her stepmother, Alice Ghostly and Kay Ballard as her stepsisters, Edie Adams as her fairy godmother and Jon Cypher as Prince Charming. The show was directed by Ralph Nelson.

Jon Cypher played the prince and Howard Lindsay his father, the king, on CBS' *Cinderella*.

THE REAL MC COYS

The unsophisticated "back home" folks, the McCoys—Grandpa, played by Walter Brennan; his son and daughter-in-law, played by Richard Crenna and Kathy Nolan; and his grandchildren, played by Lydia Reed and Michael Winkelman — were well-watched TV favorites from 1957 well into the 1960's. Mr. Brennan, playing a character similar to those he had been playing for years in many motion pictures, was his usual cantankerous old self, and the show's warmhearted humor and simple homespun philosophies kept audiences tuned in faithfully week after week.

The Real McCoys' **Tony Martinez, Lydia Reed, Walter Brennan, Michael Winkelman, Richard Crenna and Kathy Nolan.**

M SQUAD

Years before he became an Academy Award winner for his work in *Cat Ballou*, actor Lee Marvin starred in NBC's *M Squad* on television. Marvin played an elite investigator for the Chicago Police Department on the series.

Lee Marvin of the *M Squad*.

Real-life movie stars Ida Lupino and Howard Duff played make-believe movie stars Mr. Adams and Eve in a 1957 situation comedy series. Miss Lupino, who by then had earned a reputation for herself as a first-rate director, directed many of the show's sequences.

Ida Lupino and Howard Duff, a real-life husband and wife team, played Mr. Adams and Eve on television.

COLT .45

A rash of Western adventure series were seen on television in 1957. Among them were *Colt 45*, a series which starred Wayde Preston as Christopher Colt, a sharpshooting gun salesman on a secret mission for the U.S. government.

Wayde Preston of *Colt 45*.

1958

VICE PRESIDENT NIXON ON FIRST LATIN AMERICAN TOUR . . . . DE GAULLE OFFERS TO RULE FRANCE, SAYS COUNTRY FACES DISASTER WITHOUT HIM . . . . *NAUTILUS*, FIRST U.S. ATOMIC SUB, CRUISES NORTH POLE . . . . SOVIETS LAUNCH SPUTNIK III AND LEAD SPACE RACE . . . . MIDDLE EAST CRISIS INVOLVES U.S. TROOPS IN LEBANON . . . . ALASKA BECOMES THE 49TH STATE . . . .

. . . and on TV . . .

George Montgomery, who had starred in innumerable motion-picture Westerns, added television to his accomplishments when he appeared in NBC's *Cimarron City* series. Mr. Montgomery played ranch owner Matt Rockford, who fought badmen of the plains in defense of his prosperous ranch.

George Montgomery fights villain Dan Duryea on a *Cimarron City* telecast.

LAWMAN

The Western town of Laramie was the setting for ABC's *Lawman* series, which starred John Russell as the town's sheriff, Dan Troop, and Peter Brown as his deputy, Johnny McKay.

John Russell and Peter Brown of *Lawman*.

BAT MASTERSON

The Beau Brummel of the TV Western heroes, Bat Masterson, sashayed his way across TV screens for the first time on NBC in October, 1958. The well-dressed Mr. Masterson, played by Gene Barry, was a gentleman of the old school, from the tip of his shining patent-leather shoes to the pearl handle of his walking stick and the broad-brimmed Stetson. Undoubtedly Mr. Barry's Masterson characterization was the first Western marshal to be pictured as if he had just stepped out of a men's fashion magazine, *circa* 1880, and the public loved the whole idea.

Gene Barry as Bat Masterson.

MAN WITH A CAMERA

ABC's adventure-packed *Man with a Camera* series, which was about a young free-lance photographer, Mike Kovaks, starred Charles Bronson as Kovaks. Similar to radio's old *Casey, Crime Photographer* series, *The Man with a Camera* proved that photography could be dangerous, as well as fun.

The Man with a Camera, Charles Bronson.

THE UNTOUCHABLES

The crime careers of some of America's better-known mobsters were faithfully reproduced in the CBS *Untouchables* series. The show was first seen as a two-part presentation on *The Desilu Playhouse*. The public, fascinated with the authenticity of the program, asked for more, and a regular series followed. Robert Stack starred as the FBI's Eliot Ness.

Detectives Keenan Wynn and Robert Stack of *The Untouchables*.

THE DONNA REED SHOW

Academy Award-winning actress Donna Reed starred in a weekly situation-comedy series about a young doctor and his wife on *The Donna Reed Show*. Appearing with Miss Reed was Carl Betz as her doctor husband.

Carl Betz and Donna Reed of *The Donna Reed Show.*

OPEN END

David Susskind's controversial interview show *Open End* was seen on WNTA in 1958. On this "let's get together and talk" show, David "argued" with such notables as Nikita Khrushchev, Shelley Winters, Harry Belafonte, Sidney Poitier and Anthony Franciosa.

Open End's host, David Susskind.

Steve McQueen's first starring role was as Josh Randall on the CBS Western series *Wanted—Dead or Alive*. Playing a bounty hunter, Mr. McQueen and his sawed-off 30-40 carbine shotgun, which he lovingly called Mare's Laig, became TV celebrities in the late 1950's.

Steve McQueen, his shotgun "Mare's Laig" and Judith Ames on *Wanted—Dead or Alive.*

SEA HUNT

Capitalizing on the scuba diving craze of the late 1950's, CBS presented a weekly half hour series about a skin-diving soldier of fortune, Mike Nelson, played by actor Lloyd Bridges. The series had had a long, if wet, TV run before it surfaced again on re-runs.

The star of *Sea Hunt,* Lloyd Bridges.

AN EVENING WITH FRED ASTAIRE

October, 1958, marked the long-awaited television debut of the movies' King of Dance, Fred Astaire. His television dancing partner for his *Evening with Fred Astaire Show* appearance was Barrie Chase. The show and Miss Chase were such a sensation that several other Fred Astaire specials followed.

Fred Astaire and his TV dancing partner, Barrie Chase.

179

PETER GUNN

To the tune of Henry Mancini's jazzy background music, TV detective Peter Gunn worked his way to the top of the TV charts. Cool Mr. Gunn, played by actor Craig Stevens, was given ample support by Lola Albright as his girlfriend and Herschel Bernardi as his ally in the Police Department. Not long after the show's 1958 premiere, "The Theme from Peter Gunn" became a million-record hit.

Craig Stevens as Peter Gunn with Lola Albright and Herschel Bernardi.

77 SUNSET STRIP

Give a TV series a glamorous Hollywood setting, two handsome private detectives, and a good-looking teen-age idol, and what do you have? The hit TV show *77 Sunset Strip*. The two private eyes were played by Efrem Zimbalist, Jr., and Roger Smith, and the teen-age idol was Edd "Kookie" Byrnes.

Edd "Kookie" Byrnes, Roger Smith and Efrem Zimbalist of *77 Sunset Strip*.

SHIRLEY TEMPLE'S STORYBOOK

The dimpled darling baby star of the movies in the 1930's Shirley Temple made her TV debut as a full-grown but still dimpled and darling woman on a weekly series of favorite fairy tales in 1958. Each week hostess Shirley opened her oversized storybook and introduced TV viewers to a full hour of television adaptations of such favorite stories as *Beauty and the Beast, Rumpelstiltskin, The Emperor's New Clothes* and *The Little Lame Prince.* Shirley starred in two of the plays: *The Legend of Sleepy Hollow* and *Mother Goose.* The NBC series closed its storybook for the last time in June, 1959.

Shirley Temple.

LEONARD BERNSTEIN CONCERTS

Handsome, flamboyant New York Philharmonic conductor Leonard Bernstein became a television celebrity when he presented his Philharmonic concerts over the CBS network in 1958. Viewers were immediately drawn to the leonine leader who had a dramatic way with a baton and his dashing, podium postures. The success of the program led to more television appearances by Mr. Bernstein, the most notable of which being his popular *Young People's Concerts.*

Philharmonic conductor Leonard Bernstein on the podium.

TELEVISION PROGRAMS

COLOR TELEVISION: Sunday, Monday, Tuesday

Today		Monday	Tuesday
7:30—Northwest Passage (4).	9—Dinah Shore Show (4).	2:30—Haggis Baggis (4).	2:30—Haggis Baggis (4).
8—Steve Allen Show (4).		7:30—Tic Tac Dough (4).	8—Eddie Fisher Show (4).
		9:30—Hall of Fame (4).	

TV Channels

Channel 2..WCBS-TV	Channel 7..WABC-TV
Channel 4..WRCA-TV	Channel 9..WOR-TV
Channel 5..WNEW-TV	Channel 11..WPIX
Channel 13.........WNTA-TV	

TODAY, SUNDAY, OCTOBER 12

10:30-11 A. M.—Look Up and Live: "Pope Pius XII: The Man, the Office"—Jim Bishop, narrator—(2).

10-10:30 A. M.—Lamp Unto My Feet: Scenes from Sophocles' "Antigone," with Kim Hunter, Luther Adler—(2).

10:30-11 A. M.—Look Up and Live: "Vessel of Wrath"—(2).

10:30-11 A. M.—Look Up and Live: "Pope Pius XII: The Man, the Office"—Jim Bishop, narrator—(2).

11-11:30 A. M.—U. N. in Action—(2).

11-11:30 A. M.—Citizens Union Searchlight: Michael Pendergast, Democratic state chairman, interviewed—(4).

11:30-11:55 A. M.—Camera Three: "Thanks to Thurber," selections from works of James Thurber, humorist. With Elliott Nugent, the Bil and Cora Baird puppets, Hiram Sherman, Paul Trueman and others—(2).

11:30 A. M.—Noon—Report From America: "American Air Safety"—(4).

12-12:30—Eye on New York: Bill Leonard reporting—(2).

12:30-1—The New York Times Youth Forum: "Can Small Nations Help Maintain Peace?"—Ambassador Frederick H. Boland, Permanent Representative of Ireland to the United Nations, guest. Dorothy Gordon is the moderator—(4).

12:30-1—They Speak for Themselves: Science program (Première)—(4).

12:30-1—Between the Lines—(5).

1:30-2—The Catholic Hour: Part I of dramatic trilogy, "The Double Life of Christopher Mann," by Richard J. Crean, tracing the spiritual development of a young Catholic business man—(4).

1:30—College News Conference: Secretary of the Interior Fred A. Seaton—(7).

2—Pro Football: Redskins-Giants—(2).

2-2:30—The Open Mind: "Television and the Courtroom," panel discussion. Richard D. Heffner, moderator—(4).

3:30—Pro Basketball: Hawks-Warriors—(4).

3:30-4:30—Roller Derby (Première)—(5).

4:30-5—Comment: "The Jet Age," Martin Agronsky interviews authorities and reaction from homeowners reported—(4).

5-5:30—The Great Game of Politics: Samuel Lubell interviews New Yorkers on voting trends. Eric Sevareid, host—(2).

5-5:30—Frontiers of Faith: Final episode of "The Rainy Season," concerning problems of old age and retirement—(4).

5-5:30—Paul Winchell (Première)—(7).

5:30-6—Face the Nation: V. K. Krishna Menon, India's Defense Minister, interviewed in New York—(2).

5:30—Youth Wants to Know: Filmed interview with Dr. Victor M. Zhdanov, Soviet Deputy Minister of Health—(4).

6-6:30—Small World: Four-way conversation with Prime Minister Nehru of India, Aldous Huxley, British novelist; Thomas E. Dewey and Edward R. Murrow. The program is a blending of television film, overseas radio and long-distance telephone techniques (Première)—(2).

6-6:30—Meet the Press: Meade Alcorn, chairman of the Republican National Committee, interviewed—(4).

6:30-7:30—"Swiss Family Robinson," adaptation, with Laraine Day, Walter Pidgeon, Patty Duke, Dennis Kohler, Dennis Hopper—(4).

6:30—Notre Dame vs. Army—(13).

7-7:30—Lassie: With Jon Provost—(2).

7:30—Northwest Passage: Keith Larsen in "The Bound Women," with Angie Dickinson, Rebecca Welles (Color)—(4).

8:5-8:30—Maverick: "Belcastle Brand," Western, with James Garner—(7).

7:45-8:15—Governor Meyner Reports: "Workmen's Compensation," pro and con—(13).

8-9—Ed Sullivan Show: Carol Channing, Genevieve, French vocalist; Nora Kaye

8-9—Steve Allen Show: Lloyd Bridges, Larry Daniels, comedian; Carol Simpson, vocalist, guests (Color)—(4).

9-9:30—Play: "The Castaway," Western drama, with Ronald Reagan as Captain Whitney, head of a wagon train—(2).

9-10—Dinah Shore with Jimmy Durante, Julius LaRosa, Peter Lawford and Ella Fitzgerald, guests (Color)—(4).

9:30-10—Alfred Hitchcock Presents: "Don't Interrupt," with Chill Wills as a genial old rancher—(2).

9:30-10:30—Encounter: "End of Summer," a modern version of Ivan Turgeniev's short story, "Summer Love." With Hildegarde Rossi, Donald Pope and others, direct from Canada—(7).

10-10:30—The $64,000 Question: Hal March is host—(2).

10-10:30—Loretta Young Show: "For Better or for Worse," a newly elected Governor reviews case of convicted lawyer. With Edward Binns, Mark Stevens—(4).

10:30-11—What's My Line: John Daly, moderator, with Arlene Francis, Bennett Cerf, Dorothy Kilgallen and guest panelist—(2).

10:30-Movie Four: "Rebecca" (1940), with Laurence Olivier, Joan Fontaine, George Sanders, Judith Anderson. A wealthy Englishman's second marriage is overshadowed by memories of his first wife, who died—(4).

10:30-11—President Eisenhower Talk and other ceremonies at cornerstone-laying for the first national headquarters building of Protestant and Eastern Orthodox churches, in New York City (Film)—(7).

11:15-1:15—Late Show: "All Quiet on the Western Front" (1931), World War I story. With Lew Ayres, John Wray and Louis Wolheim—(2).

MONDAY, OCTOBER 13

6:30-7 A. M.—Sunrise Semester: "Classical Civilization H-1" (Monday, Wednesday and Friday)—(2).

6:30-7 A. M.—Continental Classroom: College credit course in physics (through Friday)—(4).

7-7:30 A. M.—Sunrise Semester: "Mathematics N-1," an introduction (Monday, Wednesday and Friday)—(2).

9-11 A. M.—Day in Court: Re-creations of civil and criminal court actions (through Friday) (Première)—(7).

11:30 A. M.-12:30—Peter Lind Hayes, with Mary Healy and guests in program of songs, music, informal conversation and interviews (through Friday) (Première)—(7).

12:30-1—Mother's Day: Panel show about homemaking. With Dick Van Dyke, host (through Friday) (Première)—(7).

1-1:30—The Liberace Show (through Friday) (Première)—(7).

2-2:30—Chance for Romance: With John Cameron Swayze, host (through Friday) (Première)—(7).

3-3:30—Beat the Clock: Stunt show, with Bud Collyer, host (through Friday) (Première)—(7).

7—Movie Night: "I Am a Fugitive" (1932), with Paul Muni. Unjustly convicted, a man escapes from prison but not the law (repeat 9 and 11)—(13).

7:30-8—Name That Tune: Musical quiz, with George de Witt, host—(7).

7:30-8—Tic Tac Dough: Quiz (Color)—(4).

7:30-9—Million Dollar Movie: "Godzilla," (1956), sea monster terrifies the world. With Raymond Burr and others (repeated at 10:30 and through Friday)—(9).

8-8:30—The Texan: Rory Calhoun in "Troubled Town," Western series—(2).

8-8:30—Restless Gun: Western, with John Payne in "Thunder Valley"—(4).

8:30-9—Father Knows Best: Bud discovers some startling facts about his father's high school days. With Robert Young, Billy Gray, Jane Wyatt—(2).

8:30-9—Tales of Wells Fargo: Dale Robertson in "Butch Cassidy"—(4).

8:30-9—Bold Journey: A visit to the United States "Little Diomede" Island, separated by two miles of ice and water from Russia's Big Diomede Island—(7).

8:30-9—Flight: "Show of Force," a demonstration of S. A. C. capability for immediate and heavy striking power—(11).

9-9:30—Danny Thomas Show: Comedy—(2).

9-9:30—Concert: The Philadelphia Orchestra, with Eugene Ormandy, conductor, and Hilda Gueden, soprano, soloist. John Daly is the annotator—(7).

9:30-10—Ann Sothern Show: Comedy—(2).

9:30-11—Hall of Fame: "Johnny Belinda," Ted Apstein's adaptation of the Elmer Harris play about a girl mute whose life is changed by a doctor's love. With Julie Harris, Christopher Plummer, Victor Jory (Color)—(4).

10-11—Desilu Playhouse: "Bernadette," drama of the young peasant girl and the Miracle of Lourdes. It is based on Margaret Gray Blanton's biography, "The Miracle of Bernadette." Pier Angeli will have the lead role (Première)—(2).

11:15-1:45—Late Show: "The Yearling" (1947), with Gregory Peck, Jane Wyman, Claude Jarman Jr. The story of a lonely boy and his pet baby fawn —(2).

TUESDAY, OCTOBER 14

6:30-7 A. M.—Sunrise Semester: "English H-5," great books course (Tuesday and Thursday)—(2).

7-7:30 A. M.—Sunrise Semester: "Government S-1" (Tuesday, Thursday)—(2).

7-7:30—Union Pacific: With Jeff Morrow in "Yesterday's Killers"—(7).

7-7:30—This Is Alice: Family situation comedy, with Patty Ann Garrity—(13).

7:30-8—Dragnet: With Jack Webb—(4).

7:30-8—Sugarfoot: Western series, with Will Hutchins in "The Wizard"—(7).

8:30—Keep Talking: Panel show, with Carl Reiner, host—(2).

8-9—Eddie Fisher, with Betty Hutton, Red Buttons, guests (Color)—(4).

8:30-9—To Tell the Truth: Panel show, with Bud Collyer, host—(2).

8:30-9—Wyatt Earp: "The Mysterious Cowhand," with Hugh O'Brian—(7).

9-9:30—Arthur Godfrey Show—(2).

9-10—Bob Hope, with Joan Crawford, Fernandel, French comedian; the Bernard Brothers, mimics, guests—(4).

9:30-10—Red Skelton Show—(2).

9:30-10—The Naked City: Story of a detective and his conscience after his first killing in the "Line of Duty." With James Franciscus, Diane Ladd—(7).

9:30-10:30—Harness Racing: Yonkers—(9).

10-11—Garry Moore Show: With Tommy Sands, vocalist; Audrey Meadows, Marion Lorne, comediennes; Andy Devine, guests—(2).

10-10:30—Pro Football Highlights of weekend games—(11).

11-Midnight—Open End: David Susskind, television producer, interviews guests and comments on topics of current interest (Première)—(13).

11:15-12:45—Late Show: "The Black Angel" (1946), murder mystery. With Dan Duryea, June Vincent, Peter Lorre—(2).

9:30—(2) My Little Margie (R)
(7) Film: He Stayed for Breakfast (1940), with Melvyn Douglas (R)
9:30★(11) Spanish—Grades 1-6

10:00—(2) For Love or Money
(4) Dough Re-Mi
(5) Film: Great Dan Patch (1949), With Dennis O'Keefe (R)

10:10—(11) Mathematics—Grade 9
10:30—(2) Play Your Hunch
(4) Treasure Hunt
(9) Joe Franklin
11:00—(2) Arthur Godfrey Time
(4) The Price Is Right
★(7) Day in Court
(11) Science—Grade 2
11:30—(11) English—Grade 12

1:00—(4) Our Miss Brooks
1:30—(2) As the World Turns
(4) Film Play
(5) Film: Great Dan Patch
(7) Joe Franklin
(11) Music—Grades 5-6
2:00—(2) Jimmy Dean Show
(4) Truth or Consequences
★(7) Chance for Romance
(11) Physics—Grade 11
(13) Film: Three Weird Sisters (R)
2:30—(2) Art Linkletter
(4) Haggis Baggis (C)
(7) I Married Joan (R)
(11) Almanac
3:00—(2) The Big Pay-Off
(4) Today Is Ours
(5) Film Play: Bell for Okinawa (R)

4:30—(2) The Edge of Night
(4) County Fair
(7) Mr. District Attorney (R)
(11) Spotlight on Youth
4:45—(4) Magic Clown
5:00—(4) Life of Riley (R)
(4) Movie Four: They Dare Not Love (1941), With George Brent (R)
(9) Looney Tunes
(11) Abbott and Costello
(13) Hour of Stars (R)
5:30—(2) Early Show—Film: Boom Town (1940), With Clark Gable (R)
(7) Mickey Mouse Club
(9) Mystery Theatre (R)
(11) The Three Stooges
6:00—(5) Bugs Bunny
(7) Little Rascals

(9) Terrytoon Circus
(11) News; Weather
★(13) Movie Night
7:15—(2) News Reports
(11) News Reports
7:30★(2) Name That Tune
★(4) Tic Tac Dough (C)
(5) African Patrol
(7) Jubilee U. S. A.
(9) Million Dollar Movie
(11) Amos 'n' Andy (R)
8:00★(2) The Texan
★(4) Restless Gun
(5) Follow That Man, With Ralph Bellamy (R)
(9) Whirlybirds
8:30★(2) Father Knows Best
★(4) Tales of Wells Fargo
(5) Confidential File (R)
★(7) Bold Journey
★(11) Flight

9:00—(7) Racket Squad (R)
(9) News—Jim Daly
(9) Million Dollar Movie
(11) Navy Log (R)
10:45—(11) Weather Girl
10:50—(17) Ben Hecht
11:00—(2) News; Weather; Sports
(4) News and Weather
(5) Five Star Movie: U-Boat Prisoner (1944) (R)
★(11) News Reports
11:15★(2) Late Show—Film
(4) Jack Paar Show
(7) Shock Theatre: Son of Dracula (1943), With Lon Chaney (R)
(11) Hour of Stars (R)
12:00—(9) News Reports
1:00—(4) Aqui Se Habla Ingles (R)
1:45—(2) Late Late Show—Film: Hell Below (1933), With Robert Montgomery (R)

WEDNESDAY, OCTOBER 15

5-6:30—Movie Four: "Girl in the Picture," with Donald Houston, Patrick Holt. Murder mystery is solved through clues in a snapshot—(4).

5:30-6:55—Early Show: "Dragon Fly Squadron" (1954), with John Hodiak, Barbara Britton. The training of Korean student pilots for war—(2).

7—Movie Night: "In Old Chicago" (1938), with Tyrone Power, Alice Faye. Story about the fire in 1871 (repeated at 9 and 11)—(13).

7:30-8—MacKenzie's Raiders: With Richard Carlson (Premiere)—(2).

7:30-8:30—Wagon Train: "The Jennifer Churchill Story," with Rhonda Fleming.

Robert Horton in Western romance—(4).

7:30-8:30—Lawrence Welk Show—(7).

8-9—"Dead of Noon": Repeat performance, with Richard Boone, Cameron Prud'homme in a story about the notorious gunman, John Wesley Hardin—(2).

8:30-9—The Price Is Right: Quiz, with Bill Cullen, host (Color)—(4).

8:30-9—Ozzie and Harriet: "A Surprise for Clara," family series—(7).

9-9:30—Milton Berle Show: Gary Crosby is a guest (Color)—(4).

9-9:30—Donna Reed Show: The humorous adventures of doctor's family—(4).

9-9:30—I've Got a Secret: Panel show, with Garry Moore, host—(2).

9:30-10—Bat Masterson: Gene Barry in "A Noose Fits Anybody"—(4).

9:30-10—Divorce Hearing: Dr. Paul Popenoe advises couples—(5).

9:30-10—Patti Page, with Private Steve Lawrence, guest—(7).

10-11—Ginger Rogers Show: Ray Bolger, guest (Premiere)—(2).

10—Boxing: Gil Turner vs. Ralph Dupas, welterweight bout, Montreal—(7).

11:15-1:30—Late Show: "The Corn Is Green" (1945), with Bette Davis as school teacher who befriends and encourages a poor but brilliant student who wants to attend Oxford University.

THURSDAY, OCTOBER 16

7-7:30—Tugboat Annie: "Psychologist," with Minerva Urecal and others—(7).

7-7:30—Danger Is My Business: "The Lion Trainer," Dick Walker—(13).

7:30-8—Leave It to Beaver: Comedy. "Ward's Problem," with Jerry Mathers—(7).

8-8:30—December Bride: Situation comedy, with Spring Byington—(2).

8-8:30—Ed Wynn Show: With the famous comedian as a widower who enjoys being a good samaritan—(4).

8-8:30—Zorro: Adventure, with Guy Williams in "Zorro Rides Alone"—(7).

8-8:30—Gags to Riches: With panel of comedians and Joey Adams, host—(13).

8:30-9:30—"Little Women": Richard Adler's musical version of Louisa Alcott's novel about the March family. With Margaret O'Brien, Florence Henderson, Jeannie Carson, Risë Stevens, Zina Bethune, Bill Hayes, Joel Grey and Roland Winters—(2).

8:30-9—Twenty One: Quiz, Jack Barry—(4).

8:30-9—The Real McCoys: Comedy, "Blow the House Down," with Walter Brennan, others—(7).

9-9:30—Behind Closed Doors: Counter-spy story, with Reginald Gardiner—(4).

9-9:30—Pat Boone Show—(7).

9-10:30—Jazz Party: Art Ford, host—(5).

9:30-11—Playhouse 90: "The Long March," adapted by Roger O. Hirson from the

novel by William Styron. Drama about the conflicts between veteran military officers and reservists recalled to active duty during the Korean war. With Sterling Hayden, Jack Carson, Rod Taylor, Mona Freeman—(2).

9:30-10—Tennessee Ernie Ford—(4).

10-10:30—Groucho Marx Show—(4).

10-10:30—Traffic Court: Re-creation of courtroom cases—(7).

10:30-11—Masquerade Party: Panel show, with Bert Parks, host (Color)—(4).

11:15-12:45—Late Show: "The Oklahoma Kid," with James Cagney, Humphrey Bogart in Western drama—(4).

11:15—Shock Theatre: "House of Frankenstein" (1945), with Boris Karloff—(7).

FRIDAY, OCTOBER 17

7—Movie Night: "Colorado Territory" (1949), Western, with Joel McCrea (repeated at 9 and 11)—(13).

7:30-8—Your Hit Parade: Dorothy Collins, Johnny Desmond, hosts; Tommy Edwards and the Kirby Stone Four are guests—(2).

8-9—New Adventures of Ellery Queen: With George Nader (Color)—(4).

8-9—Walt Disney Presents: "Four Down and Five Lives to Go," exploits of Elfego Baca, New Mexico lawman—(7).

8:30-9—Jackie Gleason with Buddy Hackett, comedy and music—(2).

9-9:30—Phil Silvers Show: "Bilko: The Potato Sack King," comedy—(2).

9-10—Fred Astaire, with the Jonah Jones quartet, David Rose orchestra and Barrie Chase, dancer, guests (Color) (Premiere)—(4).

9-9:30—Man With a Camera: Adventure, with Charles Bronson in "The Warning"—(7).

9:30-10—Playhouse: "The Four," with Anne Baxter. Pupils try to force a schoolteacher to resign—(7).

9:30-10:30—77 Sunset Strip: "Lovely Lady, Pity Me," about a blackmail scheme. With Efrem Zimbalist Jr., Kathleen Crowley and others—(7).

10-10:30—The Lineup: "The Missing Cargo Case," with Warner Anderson, Tom Tully in detective roles—(2).

10—Boxing: Pat McMurtry vs. George Chuvalo, heavyweight bout, from Madison Square Garden—(4).

10-11—Divorce Court: Re-creation of courtroom cases—(11).

10:30-11—Person to Person: Vincent Price and his wife, Mary, and Mata and Hari, husband-and-wife dance team are visited by Edward R. Murrow—(2).

11:15-1:30—Late Show: "Cass Timberlane" (1948), with Spencer Tracy, Lana Turner in marital drama—(2).

SATURDAY, OCTOBER 18

7-7:30 A. M.—Sunrise Semester: "English H-5," great books course—(2).

7:30-8 A. M.—Sunrise Semester: "Government S-1"—(2).

9:30-10:30 A. M.—Captain Kangaroo—(2).

2—Pro Hockey: Chicago Black Hawks vs. Detroit Red Wings—(2).

4:30-5—Horse Racing: The Jockey Club Gold Cup, from Belmont—(2).

5-6—All-Star Golf, from Miami—(7).

7:30-8:30—Perry Mason and "The Case of the Curious Bride," with Raymond Burr, Barbara Hale—(2).

7:30-8—Dick Clark Show: Julius LaRosa, Sonny James and other guests—(7).

8-9—Perry Como, with Ralph Bellamy, Eydie Gorme, vocalist; Gretchen Wyler, dancer; Robin Luke, vocalist, guests (Color)—(4).

8-9—Billy Graham's Charlotte Crusade—(7).

8:30-9—Wanted—Dead or Alive: With Steve McQueen as bounty hunter—(2).

9-10—Jerry Lewis, with Helen Traubel, soprano; Weire brothers, comedy trio, guests (Color) (Premiere)—(4).

9-10—Lawrence Welk Show—(7).

9:30-10—Have Gun, Will Travel: Paladin regrets his teaching. With Richard Boone, Peter Breck—(2).

10-10:30—Gunsmoke: Matt Dillon believes a well-groomed stranger in town is a horse thief. With James Arness—(2).

10-11—Cimarron City: "Terror Town," with Dan Duryea, George Montgomery—(4).

10-10:30—Sammy Kaye's Music—(7).

11—Cerebral Palsy Benefit Show (continued through 4:30 P. M. Sunday)—(9).

11:15-1:15—Late Show: "Shine On Harvest Moon" (1944), romantic story. With Ann Sheridan, Dennis Morgan—(2).

─── ★ *Denotes programs of unusual interest above. (C) Denotes color. (R) Denotes repeat performance.* ───

7:00★(2) Sunrise Semester
7:30★(2) Sunrise Semester
(4) Modern Farmer
8:00—(2) Big Picture
(7) Cartoon Festival
8:30—(2) U. N. Review
(7) Andy's Gang
8:45—(7) Laurel and Hardy (R)
9:00—(4) On the Carousel
(5) Children's Theatre
(7) Cartoons
9:30★(2) Captain Kangaroo
10:00—(4) Howdy Doody
(5) Films
(13) Funderama
10:30—(2) Mighty Mouse
(4) Ruff and Ready
11:00—(2) Heckle and Jeckle (R)
(4) Fury (R)
(7) Film: He Stayed For Breakfast (R)
11:30—(2) Robin Hood (R)
(4) Circus Boy
11:45—(9) Screening the World
(13) Magic Clown
12:00—(2) Film: Angel and the Badman (1947) with John Wayne (R)
(4) True Story
(5) Film: Black Glove (1954) (R)

(7) The Bontemps
(9) Janet Dean (R)
(11) Through the Porthole
(13) Gashouse Gang
12:15—(11) Industry On Parade
12:30—(4) Detective's Diary
(9) Life with Elizabeth (R)
(11) Bowling
1:00—(4) Hopalong Cassidy
(7) Foreign Legionnaire (R)
(9) O. Henry Playhouse
(11) Pro Football Highlights
(13) Film: Catwomen of the Moon (1953) with Sonny Tufts (R)
1:30—(2) Right Now
(4) To be announced
(5) Ranch Party
(7) Film: Her Husband's Affairs (1947) with Lucille Ball
(9) Million Dollar Movie
(11) Halls of Ivy (R)
2:00★(2) Pro Hockey
(7) Film: Harpoon (1948), (R)
(11) Tracer (R)
2:30—(11) Tomahawk (R)
(11) Pursuit
3:00—(11) Adventure Play-house

3:30—(5) Wanted
(7) Shock Matinee: Night Monster (1942), with Bela Lugosi (R)
4:00—(5) Film: Renegade Girl (1946), with Alan Curtis (R)
(11) Western Theatre
(13) Gunfire
4:30★(2) Horse Racing
(5) Life of Reilly (R)
(9) Charlie Chan Film (R)
★(7) All-Star Golf
(11) Laurel and Hardy
(13) Gunslingers
5:30—(5) Lone Ranger
6:00—(5) To Be Announced
(7) Rin Tin Tin (R)
(9) Buccaneers (R)
(11) Sheena (R)
(13) Dance Contest
6:30—(5) Funnytoons
(7) Annie Oakley
(9) Farmer Alfalfa
(11) Brave Eagle (R)
6:45—(9) News and Weather
7:00—(2) Target
(4) To Be Announced
(4) Range Rider (R)
(9) Jungle Jim
(11) Terrytown Circus
(11) Sky King (R)

(13) Dan Duryea Casebook
7:30★(2) Perry Mason
(4) People Are Funny (R)
(7) Douglas Fairbanks Theatre (R)
★(7) Dick Clark Show
(9) Film: Since You Went Away (1944), with Claudette Colbert (R)
(11) Jeff Collie (R)
(13) Film: Desert Victory (R)
8:00★(4) Perry Como Show (C)
(7) Mickey Rooney Show (C)
★(7) Billy Graham
(11) Film: Alexander Graham Bell, with Don Ameche (R)
8:30★(2) Wanted—Dead or Alive
(5) Mr. and Mrs. North (R)
9:00—(4) Gale Storm Show
★(5) Jerry Lewis Show (C)
(5) See the Press
(7) Lawrence Welk Show
(13) Wrestling
9:30★(2) Have Gun, Will Travel
(4) Crowded Paradise (1956), with Nancy Kelly (R)
(11) Guy Lombardo

10:00★(2) Gunsmoke
★(4) Cimarron City
★(7) Sammy Kaye's Music
(9) Bowling
(11) Film: Les Miserables, with Frederic March (R)
(13) Jungle
10:30—(2) Sea Hunt
(7) Shock Theatre (R)
11:00—(2) News; Weather; Sports
(4) News Reports
(5) Five Star Movie: Passport to Pimlico (1949) (R)
★(9) Cerebral Palsy Benefit
(13) Film: Long Voyage Home (1940), with John Wayne (R)
11:10—(11) Sports and Weather
11:15★(2) Late Show
(4) Movie Four: The Red Pony (1948), with Robert Mitchum (R)
(11) Film: Twist of Fate (1954), with Ginger Rogers (R)
1:15—(2) Late Late Show: Lady in the Lake (1947), with Robert Montgomery (R)

WATCH this fabulous new line-up of live DAYTIME TV shows starting tomorrow on WABC-TV CHANNEL 7

DAY IN COURT

Ordinary citizens come to trial on charges that could be brought against you! New cases daily.

11:00 - 11:30 A. M.

CHANCE FOR ROMANCE

John Cameron Swayze pairs off adult men and women—screened by expert psychologists!

2:00 - 2:30

THE PETER LIND HAYES SHOW

Peter struts and mimics his way through a hilarious full hour! Mary Healy is guest star!

11:30 - 12:30

BEAT THE CLOCK

Laughs come fast as contestants vie in uproarious races against time. Bud Collyer MC's.

3:00 - 3:30

MOTHER'S DAY

Compare your homemaking skills with those of our prize-winning moms! Host: Dick Van Dyke!

12:30 - 1:00

WHO DO YOU TRUST?

The funniest comedy quiz on TV — engineered by Funnyman First Class Johnny Carson!

3:30 - 4:00

THE LIBERACE SHOW

Intimate new song stylings, played (and sung!) by a new Liberace! He sings to one woman, you!

1:00 - 1:30

MONDAY THROUGH FRIDAY

DAYTIME TV MEANS WABC-TV CHANNEL 7

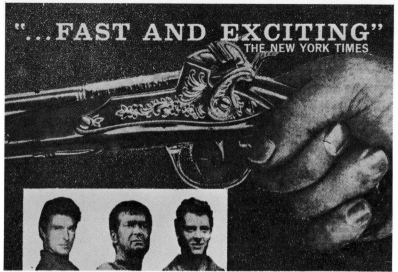

"...FAST AND EXCITING"
THE NEW YORK TIMES

NORTHWEST PASSAGE. The drama of America's early days comes excitingly alive, as Keith Larsen, Buddy Ebsen and Don Burnett star in another trail-blazing adventure of Major Rogers and his rough-and-ready Indian-fighting Rangers. In Color and black and white.
TONIGHT AT 7:30 ON NBC 4

STEVE ALLEN

JUDY HOLLIDAY EXTRA ADDED ATTRACTION LLOYD BRIDGES
comedian Larry Daniels and singing sensation Carol Simpson join forces with the fun-loving Allen All-Stars on tonight's high-spirited STEVE ALLEN SHOW. Live and lively in Color and black and white.
TONIGHT 8:00-9:00 ON NBC 4

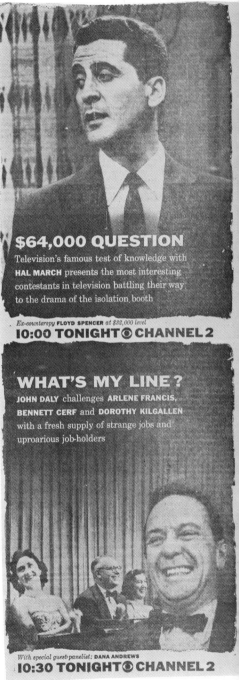

TV SPORTSCASTERS

Marty Glickman

Harry Wismer

Tommy Harmon

Ted Husing

Leo Durocher

Red Barber

Red Grange

Bud Palmer

Mel Allen

INDEX

188

189

190